# LOOKING AHEAD

## A PERSONAL THEOLOGY OF HOPE

CHARLES LEE HOLLAND JR.

Printed in the United States of America

| Library of Congress Control Number: | 2019917221 |
|---|---|
| ISBN:Softcover | 978-1-64376-525-9 |
| Hardcover | 978-1-64376-526-6 |
| eBook | 978-1-64376-524-2 |

Republished by: PageTurner, Press and Media LLC
Publication Date: November 14, 2019

**To order copies of this book, contact:**

PageTurner, Press and Media
Phone: 1-888-447-9651
order@pageturner.us
www.pageturner.us

# CONTENTS

# PART 4

# DEDICATION

**In memory:**

*Elizabeth, Alice, and Virgil*

**Parents superior in every way.**

**In honor:**

*Jeanette C. Holland*

**Bride of my youth, love of my life, forever best friend.**

**In celebration:**

*Denise, Alicia, and Beth*

**Beloved daughters, in whom I am well-pleased.**

# PREFACE

With increasing frequency, it has become *the norm* to hear from diverse sources the declaration that we now live in a post-Christian world in which the prevailing influences include the ideologies of a pluralistic and multicultural society. So, from the perspective of a fair and balanced approach, we Christians must pay intellectual and socially correct respect to the competing and conflicting views of people of all religions, and of people who boast no religion at all. Such is the way it is in the world as it is.

Therefore, the chapters of this book are presented with the awareness that Christianity in our time confronts the crisis of the relevance of the church and the challenge facing biblical theology. The reflections recorded hereinafter are autobiographical in nature because they mirror the perspective of one who for sixty years in ministry has sought to communicate the gospel with intellectual and spiritual integrity. I remain convinced that historic Christianity must and will prevail triumphantly in this time of unparalleled testing. It is certain that, by the grace of God, we possess the means to succeed in our mission. The ultimate question for us is whether or not we possess the will to succeed.

In the preparation of this book, I have been helped by the countless significant theological and inspirational books that I have read during the years. Further, the lectures, conversations, and related publications of the outstanding professors who have guided my quest for a reasoned faith continue to influence my every thought and word. Of course, the amazing interest in biblical theology held by many parishioners in the churches I have been privileged to serve motivates the effort to produce this book. Therefore, I affirm a personal debt to many for their objective and subjective contributions, remembering that any errors inherent in the work are my own.

Most of all, I wish to thank Jeanette, my dear wife. She has often endured my lengthy discussions on this subject that is so significant to me. She has epitomized great patience with her insight, her challenges to my ideas, and her loving and never-failing encouragement.

**Charles L. Holland Jr.**

Fort Worth, Texas

Spring 2017

# PART 1

## Prologue:
# LOOKING AHEAD

# LOOKING AHEAD

It has been said that *youth longs, and mankind strives, but age remembers.* Well, I suppose. However, as the years continue to unfold in my octogenarian decade of living, I have made a significant discovery: although remembering occupies a significant measure of my reflections, I find myself looking ahead. In fact, the future continues to retain a provocative and compelling interest for me. Of course, such thinking inevitably involves the inclusion of the reality of death.

Any mention of death invites us to face the certain absolutes inherent in that eventuality. For one thing, we realize that death is a part of the human experience and has been so from the very beginning. Within the sacred mythology of the creation narrative, there is the story of Cain and Abel. We are introduced to Abel as a vibrant and active individual who quickly becomes victim to a violent death at the hands of his brother. Suddenly, he is seen as a cold and lifeless corpse that is buried and destined to become a part of the very dust that covers his body.

Of course, we may be certain that the grieving parents of Abel knew the pain and devastation of losing a greatly beloved child. Thus, we learn that the death of a person affects those who knew and loved him or her. Accordingly, the reality of death remains with us still. It is as the years multiply that one becomes increasingly aware of the terminal certitude of his or her own existence. Personally, I am discovering a quite surprising phenomenon. The notion of my personal demise does not prompt feelings of dread, anxiety, or fear. Rather, I find myself embracing a stimulating curiosity with regard to the future.

It is my desire to acquire a competent knowledge of what the future holds, not only for me, but for those whom I love as well. I want to affirm the basis for the beliefs that constitute the essential religious creed of my life. I am intrigued by the thought of life beyond life; that is to say that I am fascinated by the promise of eternal life. I am increasingly obsessed by the whole issue of essential life. For example, if indeed we are spiritual entities, and, therefore, transcend time and space, our essential lives might very well predicate our actual lives. To put it another way, I have no trouble believing in life after life, so why should I be troubled with the thought of life before life? Indeed, Plato embraced the idea of the immortality of the soul in his belief that the soul existed from all eternity. See, this has become for me a magnificent obsession. Constantly, I try to retain an open mind and an open heart so that I may be responsive to any revelation God may provide.

It is logical, at this point, to mention an important matter: *where can the answers to these provocative questions be found?* More than ever before in my life, I am increasingly convinced that the viable key to truth is composed of *reason* and *faith*. There is abundant evidence that since ancient times, people have sought to delve into the mystery of the future based on logic and reason. It is small wonder that any serious study of the wise and serious minds of the past reveals that there exist many and varied paths purported to lead to God, the ultimate destiny of humanity, and the entire universe. Obviously, with such diversity, and with no two minds of identical conclusion, an acceptable synthesis is never reached. Nevertheless, clear and objective thinking remains an important means of reaching for truth.

Then there is the component of faith. After all, it becomes clear that we are dealing with realities that prevail far beyond the limits of human knowledge. It is at this point that *faith* emerges as the singular integrating force in the quest for insight into the future. Simply stated, I remain confident that God has seen fit to provide authentic revelation of Himself as well as some of His plans for the future. The Holy Scriptures is that supreme source book to guide us in our sojourn forward into that future. It is clear to me that what our human reason has failed to clarify, divine revelation has accomplished.

It is appropriate, it seems to me, to speak of my personal view of the scriptures. After all, that view will be a determinative factor in all that I shall say hereinafter. Of course, I am aware that God has made use of human authors in the compilation of the Bible. However, I am equally confident that the divine superintendence by God of the writing process results in the unique status of the Bible. Thus, although we do not have all of the specific details pertaining to the future, both in time and eternity, we may be grateful that God has provided an insight into at least a part of what we may expect. Therefore, we may, with confidence, take what is given in the scriptures, contribute our own respectful and reverent reason, and reach meaningful conclusions. This is the essence of authentic biblical theology.

Now, I am back where I started. I live these days with a constantly growing interest in the future. However, this interest in the future is not limited to the next months or years of living in this world, this age, or this chronological sphere known as our life span. Rather, I want to know more and more and more about what I like to call the *cosmic future.* In other words, I long to understand something of God's long-range plans for me, my family, my friends, and the universe. Really, I do not believe that this is too much to ask.

Perhaps there are those persons who will wonder why such considerations are of interest to me. Well, one thing is quite certain: *the future is of interest to me because I know that one way or the other, I am going to experience the future.* The result of such reflections for me is personally quite edifying. You might say that it actually allows me to live in the light of eternity in the here and now. That is why during these days, I find myself constantly **looking ahead**.

## I.  Death and Beyond

Suppose our attitude toward death were positive rather than negative. Suppose we were able to embrace the event of death as the advent of a friend rather than the invasion of our ultimate enemy. If such were the case, we could find rest in the affirmation that death is as natural and normal as birth and is an integral component of God's sovereign plan. I realize that this may be difficult for most Christians because of our fixation on the views of St. Paul, who saw death as the penalty and punishment for our individual and collective sin:

> Therefore as through one man sin entered the world,
> and death through sin;

5

and so death passed unto all men,
for all have sinned. (Romans 5:12 KJV)

Taken at face value, these words defy clear thinking. After all, long before humans populated the earth, the reality of pain, suffering, and death among the prehistoric animals was all too common, as "red in tooth and claw" was the basic diapason of the evolutionary process. So, in contradistinction from the notion of Paul, I am coming more and more to view death not as penalty or punishment for my sin but as a blessing—not as a tragedy, but as a triumph; not as the end, but as the beginning of a transcendent experience. In this particular, I wholeheartedly endorse Paul's description of the glory waiting us "on the other side":

Yet among the mature we do speak wisdom,
though it is not a wisdom of this age or of
the rulers of this age, who are doomed to
perish. But we speak God's wisdom,
secret and hidden, which God decreed before
the ages for our glory. None of the rulers of
this age understood this, for if they had, they
would not have crucified the Lord of Glory.
But as it is written:

"What no eye has seen nor ear heard,
nor the human heart conceived,
what God has prepared for those
who love him. "(1 Corinthians 2:6–9 NRSV)

Of course, this is a positive declaration of religious faith. I know that there are many people who remain intellectually pragmatic and, so, refuse to honor conclusions drawn simply from the arena of subjective faith. In spite of talk of resurrection, they have never seen anyone who has been laid away in the grave come forth alive after death. For them, such thinking is a defiance of all reason, and they resist such a far-fetched notion. It may be said that as far as personal experience is concerned, death is factually the end. However, this never can be taken as the definitive conclusion of the matter. The discipline of pure logic stipulates that one cannot draw a universal negative conclusion from limited personal experience. By way of example, none of us living today ever saw Abraham Lincoln, but that is not proof that such a person never existed. We Christians do have a singular winning argument in that we possess historical proof that one person has come forth from the grave. That person, of course, is Jesus Christ. His post-resurrection appearances do affirm the truth that when one comes back from the grave, he does not return to share the kind of life we know. Rather, the resurrected one enters into a life of the spirit, which is altogether different from this life. To deny the life of the spirit is comparable to a blind person denying the existence of light. I realize that I have not experienced that new life as yet, but that does not abrogate the existence of the spiritual life.

It is such thinking as this that provides me with a calm confidence that death is not an exit but an entrance. That is why I find myself looking ahead! In addition, there is further affirmation of this position that has emerged through many years of ministry. I once stood by the bedside of a Christian gentleman who had experienced a devastating illness that had left him lingering in a coma for almost a week. I happened to be there with him when he awakened. As the shadows of near death began to lift, I noted a strange, new light in his eyes now opening easily. The expression of those eyes was one of great joy and happiness. Then, in an almost startling way, he reached for my hand and said, "Charles, I have seen the most beautiful place you can imagine, and I have heard the most wonderful music—I can't begin to describe it. And, Charles, I have seen Jesus." That dear man was my own grandfather, Furman Jutson Nolen. A man of limited education and descriptive vocabulary, Papa never used such language in his normal conversation. What happened? Papa was given a glimpse of God's eternity, and the language of Paul was given to him by his loving Father:

> What no eye has seen, nor ear heard, nor the human heart conceived, what God has prepared for those who love him.

For me, the summation of the matter results from a blending of reason, faith, and personal experience. Therefore, that which we call death summons the end to our physical bodies in their present form. The truly important part of us, the soul, or the spirit—that which makes us unique personalities—lives on. Death is an entrance into another and greater life; it certainly is not the end! Therefore, I keep on looking ahead!

7

## II. Two Places to Spend Eternity

The discussion of *our heavenly home* leads one whose entire adult life has been influenced by biblical theology to return inexorably to the words of scripture. There, it is made very clear that there are two places where individuals will spend eternity. One such clear passage is found in Matthew 25:31–46 (NRSV):

> When the Son of man shall come in his glory... before him shall be gathered all nations: and he shall separate them one from another, as a shepherd divides his sheep from the goats ... Then shall the King say unto them on the right hand, Come, you blessed of my Father, inherit the kingdom prepared for you from the foundation of the world ... Then shall he say to them on the left hand, Depart from me, you cursed, into everlasting fire, prepared for the devil and his angels ... And they shall go away into everlasting punishment: but the righteous into eternal life.

There are many additional passages in both the Old and New Testaments that affirm the same emphasis. It is needless to quote from other such passages here, as anyone can easily find them in abundance. Actually, when I begin contemplating the biblically indicated places for the eternal residence of "departed souls," I must admit the dismissal of rigid dogmatism from my thoughts. Frankly, because of my faith in the Father and my confidence in the mission and message of Jesus, I find thinking of Heaven to be natural, inviting, and pleasantly provocative. I intend to share my thoughts in this regard shortly. In contrast, serious and objective considerations of Hell are quite challenging to me. Therefore, I posit for myself certain essential questions:

1. Am I willing to apply the principles and methods of critical scholarship to all biblical texts?

2. Is it intellectually and spiritually legitimate to apply metaphorical and symbolic significance to the narratives, parables, and statements of the prophets, apostles, and even Jesus?

3. Am I forced to affirm that I must take literally each and every component of the scriptures and interpret them accordingly?

4. Is it appropriate to embrace the notion that many portions of the scriptures are best viewed as vehicles that bear the revealed truth of God to humankind?

I am quite willing to confess that, in many instances of textual consideration, I am what may be called a *believing agnostic,* meaning simply that I do not have the answers and I do not know. This is my attitude as I think of the biblical subject of Hell. For example, those burning and unquenchable fires of Hell, which are vividly portrayed in the Bible, beg the question, "Is this literal, or is this a symbol of a reality far greater than the symbol itself?"

We all have heard sermons on the Great Judgment that is to come and the opened book in which our deeds in life are recorded and made public. If Hell is to be our destiny, what will it be like? Is it possible that the Hell we shall know will be the Hell of our own making?

I said earlier that I am a believing agnostic. I do not have the answers to these troublesome issues. Thus, I find myself talking to myself. It is very difficult to contemplate a person existing through an endless eternity in a place of terrible pain and torture. Still, I know that unforgiven sin deserves punishment. Accordingly, would a just God treat a saintly, believing mother in exactly the same way as an Adolph Hitler? Why would anyone care to try to be good if those persons who are altogether bad receive the same treatment as those who sincerely try to be and do good? Such thoughts as these weave their way into my very psyche to the point that I simply surrender to the reality of my personal finitude and embrace my intellectual limitations in the matter. Still, it seems important to me that I attempt some effort to summarize in some measure a personal conclusion (realizing in the process that no other person may hold the same notion).

I have no idea whether or not there will be actual fire and brimstone in Hell. It is my own view that spiritual bodies would not and could not be affected by such things. I am sensitive to the words the scripture uses to describe Hell. There is talk of fire, burning sulphur, worms, the Valley of Hinnom, weeping, wailing, and gnashing of teeth. None of these things holds any attraction for me. Simply stated, I do not know if such descriptions are to be taken literally or if they are images of a form of regret and psychological suffering that are infinitely worse than the interpretive impressions of Milton and Dante. I might be tempted to accept the idea of hell as a place of punishment, a *temporary abode,* designed to house the wicked until the day of the final resurrection and judgment. Inherent in this view is the conviction that God may have plans for all humanity, the evil as well as the good, which are far beyond our capacity to comprehend at this time. I keep remembering those provocative words written by the faithful disciple of Jesus who may have known the mind of the Savior better than any other:

> The Lord is not slow about his promise, as some think of slowness, but is patient with you, not wanting any to perish, but all to come to repentance. (2 Peter 3:9 NRSV)

I mentioned that this verse is quite compelling for me. It prompts some serious, even profound, reflections. For one thing, is spiritual conversion limited to this life only? When we die, is God through working with us to develop us into the persons he intended in our creation and birth? Is it possible that a truly repentant soul may grasp the grace of God and be "saved" beyond the event of death? Even from Hell itself? I am quite willing to rest these questions in the hands of the sovereign and loving God, the Father of our Lord Jesus Christ.

Now, what about that other "place" spoken of in the Bible? What about Heaven? Although we are not given all the information about heaven we might wish, there is much more biblical material pertaining to this subject than is true of Hell. Both the Old and New Testaments are replete with references pertaining to the glorious habitat of the redeemed. And yet, there are some things we know and some things we do not know.

We are engaged in a subject that is quite beyond the realm of knowledge acquired by the exercise of our own senses. The glorious pictures of Heaven are enchanting, inviting, and alluring. How shall we interpret them? Should they be viewed as literal or figurative? Frankly, I am unwilling to apply a general statement at this point. I speak only for myself. I cannot take a dogmatic approach to this important and interesting subject. I can only apply certain deductive impressions in this regard. For one thing, the respective biblical authors had to use human language in writing about heaven. We know that human language is totally inadequate to describe transcendent and spiritual realities. One thinks of the difficulty of attempting to describe the majestic sight of Niagara Falls to a blind person, or the glorious sounds of Bach's "St. Matthew's Passion" to a deaf person.

Some of the significant efforts to provide light on the matter are as follows:

> Eye has not seen, nor ear heard, neither have entered into the heart of man the things which God has prepared for those who love him. (1 Corinthians 2:9 NRSV)

> In my Father's house there are many dwelling places. (John 14:2 NRSV)

> Truly I tell you, today you will be with me in Paradise. (Luke 23:43 NRSV)

> Then I saw a new heaven and a new earth … And I saw the holy city, the new Jerusalem, coming down out of heaven from God, prepared as a bride adorned for her husband. (Revelation 21:1–2 NRSV)

Of course, as is true of many Christians, I cherish the many anthropomorphic symbols employed to describe the bliss of eternity with God. We are told that for those persons who are tired from the toils of this life, there will be rest. I find myself wondering if I would be happy very long if I were to be relegated to some celestial rocking chair for eternity. There are further extravagant descriptions! For those persons who are sad, God himself will wipe away their tears. For the people who have suffered in poverty, Heaven will be the place where even the streets are paved with gold—no poverty there! And for all those persons who wish they could sing, there will be heavenly choirs, and we all will be endowed with golden voices with which to praise God forever. Again, this comes across to me as some eternal worship service, and I keep thinking that I have already lived through enough of those everlasting worship services here on earth!

In summary, I believe in the reality of eternal life in the presence and person of God himself. Frankly, my personal impressions of Heaven are difficult for me to describe. However, I shall make an effort to share my deepest thoughts. I find it impossible to think of anything less than ultimate joy and happiness in complete bliss in the Father's House, the divinely designated eternal habitat for all humanity. It seems to me that heaven will be actualized in the transcendent experience of each believer when he or she becomes one with God, sharing in his life. All evil will have been vanquished, and each believer will realize unspeakable and unimaginable glory. This, I am convinced, is to be the final destiny of every person. Such will be a measure of the glory of God and the ultimate bliss of humankind.

I wish to make very clear one important point. Personally, I believe in the survival of the human soul (spirit) for many reasons. However, one factor is of supreme value to my thinking: *Jesus was absolutely certain of the reality of the next life and of the spiritual and eternal benefits of heaven.* Therefore, the more I reflect on the message of Jesus, the more confident I become that the entire universe is essentially spiritual. Thus, I need have no fear of physical death because it will be the welcome release of my spirit into the reality of Spirit—that is, God himself. I live now (in time) and in the future (in eternity) in the loving hands of infinite Love. He is the same divine architect who planned and arranged my physical birth so that loving and caring hands welcomed me into this life. Further, he says to me, "I go to prepare a place for you … and I will come and receive you unto myself" (John 14:2–6 KJV). In other words, I have the promise that loving and caring hands are ready to welcome me into the Father's house. To enhance our sense of security, Jesus added, "If it were not so I would have told you" (John 14:2 KJV).

Many years ago, I discovered an anonymous poem which constantly has enriched my thinking:

## Home

Think of stepping on shore, and finding it Heaven!
Of taking hold of a hand, and finding it God's hand,
Of breathing new air, and finding it celestial air,
Of feeling invigorated, and finding it immortality,
Of passing from storm and tempest to an unbroken calm,
Of waking up, and finding it Home!

So, one may wonder, why should an aging theologian/minister continue **Looking Ahead**? I continue looking ahead because that is where the future is. That is where heaven is, and I fully expect to arrive there at some point. It is there, I am confident, that I shall witness the finish of pain, travail, sorrow, doubt, and fear. It is there that I shall experience peace, rest, and calm. It is there that I shall engage in reunion with those loved ones whom I have lost for a brief while. It is there that I shall know them far better than I ever knew them in this life. Ultimately, it is there that my spirit will be joined with Spirit, and this will be final redemption and a transcendent intimacy of sublime joy. Further, it is there that I shall be prepared by God for further service and ministry in his eternal kingdom. And, I shall never be retired again! You see, I have a lot to live for and die for! *I keep looking ahead!*

# PART 2

## The Apostles' Creed:

# A CONTEMPORARY INTERPRETATION

# THE APOSTLES' CREED

I believe in God, the Father Almighty, maker of heaven and earth;

And in Jesus Christ his only Son our Lord:
who was conceived by the Holy Spirit, born of the Virgin Mary,
suffered under Pontius Pilate, was crucified, dead, and buried; the third
day he rose from the dead; he ascended into heaven,
and sitteth at the right hand of God the Father Almighty;
from thence he shall come to judge the quick and the dead.

I believe in the Holy Spirit,
       the holy Catholic church,
       the communion of saints,
       the forgiveness of sins,
       the resurrection of the body,
       and the life everlasting. Amen.

# WHY I BELIEVE in GOD

> I believe in God the Father Almighty,
> maker of heaven and earth.
> —The Apostles' Creed

For as long as I can recall, I have shared in singing about God, confessing my faith in God, praying to God, and preaching about God. As a matter of fact, I am unable to remember a time when I did not express my faith in God. To be honest, I made such affirmations in my earlier days without any significant reservations. In the passing of time, I have developed a less audacious attitude toward the subject of God. This does not imply that I have experienced a time of disbelief in the reality of God, but it does suggest that I have been willing to ask of myself why I have faith in the existence and relevance of God.

This discussion provokes a serious effort to analyze the various and multiple paths that lead a believer to a convinced faith in the reality of God. At this stage of life, my faith is the result of a combination of reason and faith. Reason continues to play a dominant role in my personal theological conclusions. It seems relevant to review how this has come to pass. Years ago, I was introduced to Rene Descartes, French mathematician and founder of modern philosophy, who provided one terse sentence that became the starting point of the science of reason: **"Ego cogito, ergo sum."** *I think, therefore I am.* The parsing of this sentence sets the stage for an intellectual approach to the subject of God. First, *I* introduces the idea of individuality, personality, and spirituality.

Next, *think* suggest the idea of life, consciousness, and mind. Then, *therefore* indicates that mind not only is conscious and thinks, it also reasons and draws inferences. Further, *am* carries the idea that existence is actual and not merely idea. Actually, this brief sentence underscores reason as a legitimate means of pursuing truth. In light of this, I have been strongly influenced by the disciplines of logic in my personal quest for knowledge of God. So, there are philosophical paths that have led me to faith in God.

## The Ontological Path

This significant path is based upon and derived from the nature of being or the fact of existence. The very first component of reason indicates that deity is drawn from the fact of existence. Simply stated, something exists, and therefore something must always have existed. The classic declaration of this argument is that out of nothing comes nothing. In other words, if ever there were a time when absolutely nothing existed, it is impossible that anything could ever have come into existence. Since I am unable to conceive of a time when nothing existed, I deduce the necessity of the existence of something—God.

## The Cosmological Path

It seems to me that this is a very strong argument for the existence of God. The cosmological argument asserts that in consideration of the orderly arrangement of the universe, both as a whole and in its respective parts, there is a recognition of the fact that nothing happens in this universe of being that is unrelated to something antecedent to it as a causative factor. God is that causative factor.

## The Teleological Path

This path leads me directly to faith in the existence of God. It argues that it is impossible that something should come into existence out of nothing. This means that it is equally impossible that there should be in the effect anything greater than the cause. Therefore, consciousness, personality, spirituality, and free will must exist, in essence, in the producing cause. That cause is God.

## The Moral Path

The innate nature of humans provides in conscience certain evidence that it came from and is related to a moral God. The ultimate decisions we make in life are not those that concern matters that are basically intellectual or emotional. Rather, the momentous decisions we make involve the matter of right and wrong—that is, moral responsibility followed by moral consequences. How did we come to be possessed of a sense of moral conscience? What makes one thing right and another thing wrong? How did we come to have within us an authoritative voice directing us to do one thing and not do another? What is the true origin of ethics? Is it genetic? Is it environmental? Is it matter? No! It is none of the aforementioned. The only rational explanation for the origin and existence of moral humans and a moral world is the existence of a moral God.

## Consensus Gentium

There remains yet what may be called the consensus argument. While it is unlike all other paths that lead to God, it includes and re-inforces all the others in that it finds a certain universality of faith in the existence of some kind of deity. From this argument, there emerges the view that such a universal and abiding conviction by the entire human race cannot be a delusion or an illusion. Thus, the synthesis ob-servation is that all logical or rational paths lead one to an intellectual acceptance of the reality of God.

## Through the Bible to God

I have been most fortunate to spend my entire adult life in a vocation that involves, by necessity, an intimate knowledge of the Bible. Therefore, for sixty years and counting, it has been my privilege to make the study of the scriptures the primary focus of my ministry. There are no words adequate to communicate the great blessing this endeavor has brought to my life. I entered the ministry many years ago, with limited knowledge about God as a result of growing up in a Christian home and a Bible-believing church. However, through the years, as I have continued to study the sacred scriptures, I have come to know God in personal faith that results in an existential relationship. I would like to share a few impressions pertaining to the ways in which the Bible has introduced me to God the Father Almighty, Creator of heaven, earth, and each of us.

With a majestic sentence of poetic grandeur, the Bible begins in a way that exceeds even inspiration: "In the beginning God created the heavens and the earth." With this profound declaration, one immediately gains the impression that the Bible is preeminently God's book. It begins and ends with God. I still can recall a favorite phrase of my seminary professor of theology, Dr. Felix Gear: "*A Deo, de Deo, in Deum*." Eventually, I asked him to translate the Latin phrase for me, to which he replied, "Charles, it is from God, concerning God, and leads to God!" I wonder if a better definition of the Bible ever has been produced. It is perhaps true that in those early years of my theological studies, I failed to grasp the profound significance of that definition. However, now at the tag end of a long ministry, I understand clearly how ultimately important the Bible has been in my life. This is the reason why biblical theology has remained the passion of my study, research, and preaching.

Allow me to press this point a bit further. I am convinced that the Bible provides us with that which history, nature, and reason cannot supply, which is an intellectually and emotionally satisfying concept of God. In addition, this biblical concept of God is so transcendent that the greatest of human minds can conceive of nothing higher or more perfect. Therefore, it becomes evident that, unique in all literature, it is in the Bible that the divine has appeared.

I am knowledgeable and conversant in the area of the so-called scientific study of the Bible. In other words, I am aware of the respective disciplines of textual criticism, literary criticism, redaction criticism, and canonical criticism, and I have utilized these disciplines throughout the years. And yet, I can declare with conviction that I believe the Bible to be the inspired Word of God. As a pastor, I have sat by the bedside of seriously ill or dying people many times. Inevitably, when I pause to read the Psalm 23 or, perhaps, John 14, I have witnessed the reality of God's living Word breathing hope and comfort into the minds and hearts of the suffering and anxious individuals. Because of such instances as this, I am convinced that the Bible is God's inspired Word to humankind. That is why I believe the Bible, I love the Bible, and I preach the Bible.

In the final analysis, pertaining to the subject of the Bible, it is not one's theory of biblical inspiration that matters, but it is the use of the Bible as a guidebook to God and a godly life that affirms the reality and authenticity of its inspiration. Surely it is true that no spiritually minded person can read the Bible without hearing the voice of God speaking to him or her. This is the way I continue to know God better and more intimately. Indeed, the Bible continues to be for me an essential path to God. The Bible—*a Deo, de Deo, in Deum*!

# WHY I BELIEVE IN JESUS CHRIST

And [I believe] in Jesus Christ his only Son our Lord:
who was conceived by the Holy Spirit,
born of the Virgin Mary,
suffered under Pontius Pilate,
was crucified dead and buried;
the third day he rose from the dead;
he ascended into heaven,
and sitteth at the right hand of God the Father Almighty;
from thence he shall come to judge the quick and the dead.
—The Apostles' Creed

Obviously, these are the words taken from the familiar Apostles' Creed. Along with other Christian congregants, these are the words I usually recite each Sunday during worship. For millions of people who are not Christians, these words are intellectually offensive or somewhat humorous. Viewed from the perspective of pure reason, they do defy logic. To me, they signify the central truth of the redemptive event determined by God for the salvation of the human race. I believe them to be true, and I joyfully proclaim them as the essence of the Christian gospel. It seems important to me that I share something of my intellectual and spiritual journey to arrive at such a strong and abiding conviction.

There is no personal recollection of a time when I did not believe in Jesus Christ. The first story I remember being read to me was from my childhood Jesus book. The first song I remember learning was "Jesus Loves Me, This I Know." I still love to sing that song because I still believe it to be true. My primal memory involves attending church and Sunday School and learning about Jesus and his many wonderful miracles. I suppose that one might conclude that I always have been a believer. It is not surprising, therefore, that I made a public profession of my faith in Jesus as God's Son and was baptized when I was eleven years of age. So it was that through childhood, adolescence, and the teenage years I retained an uncomplicated, simplistic, and non-questioning faith in Jesus..

## He Was Conceived by the Holy Spirit

As one matures in the faith, he loses the tendency of hesitating to worship God with his mind as well as with his heart. Therefore, if one thinks at all while he recites the respective creeds of his faith, there comes a moment of sudden awareness of the incredible statements integral to the confession ritual. For example, there came a moment when I confronted the strange statement in the Apostles' Creed regarding the conception of Jesus: *(He) was conceived by the Holy Spirit!* Employing the critique of pure reason, this phrase defies logic. Am I to understand that the Holy Spirit became a substitute for a human male? Does this mean that the Holy Spirit served as a sperm donator to the mother of Jesus? If such were the case, that would mean that the Holy Spirit was the actual father of Jesus! This notion instantly was repulsive to me! Such thinking would result in Jesus actually being a half-breed: half-god and half-man. Again, it seems to me that this is an absurd conclusion.

It should be remembered that there are many ancient mythologies that speak about the gods descending to have intercourse with human females, thus producing mythological half-god and half-man offspring. Certainly, this is not the nature of the incarnation narrative. Then what does this phrase really mean? Simply stated, it means that *Jesus had no father at all.* This statement in the Apostles' Creed is not to be viewed in any sense as a biological explanation. Rather, it is a declaration that a biological explanation does not exist! The conception of Jesus is to be viewed as a divine miracle. Perhaps the clearest statement of this miracle is found in the Gospel of John 1:14: "And the word became flesh." Believing in the validity of the creation "out of nothing" as taught in the book of Genesis, there is no great leap of fantasy to believe in the "creation" of the embryo within the womb of Mary by God. Paul refers to Jesus as the "second Adam." The analogy is obvious (at least for Paul), that both the first Adam and the second Adam (Jesus) were the result of the supernatural creation of God. As at the beginning, God spoke, and it was done.

My thoughts pertaining to the advent narratives have evolved over the years. I no longer view them as an adequate explanation of *how* God entered into the world as a real human man, but, rather, as a declaration that *he did* come to us in a man. In no way does such thinking abrogate the existence of the mystery of the incarnation. It is, however, an attempt to articulate, in clear terms, the essence of the Christian faith that the conception of Jesus Christ was the result of an eternal formula: God spoke, the miracle was done, and the Savior was born!

## *He Was Born of the Virgin Mary*

Generally speaking, the affirmations of the Apostles' Creed accurately define the historic Christian faith, and certainly they define my own personal faith. However, I would be less than honest if I glided past this particular part without reverent and respectful consideration. Remember that I have affirmed that I believe that the Holy Spirit was present and active in the conception of Jesus Christ. However, with reference to the statement, "He was born of the Virgin Mary," I think that additional analysis and reflection are essential.

It is the task of biblical theology to examine the scriptures themselves and make relevant interpretations based on sincere, critical, and careful reflection. With reference to the subject of the virgin birth, we are limited to two passages. If one is able to ignore the traditional rendering of the Christmas story and examine the record itself, one finds a confusing and complicated narrative. For example, consider Matthew 1:18–24. In verse 18, Mary is *betrothed* to Joseph. In verse 19, Joseph is introduced as her *husband,* and it said that he is minded to *divorce* her. In verse 20, Mary is referred to as Joseph's *wife.* Of course, it is significant to note that much of the confusion of this language is related to the prevailing custom of the day in which the marriage process involved three distinct stages: *engagement, betrothal,* and the *marriage ritual* itself. The evident explanation is that the incidents recorded in Matthew all occurred during the year of betrothal. That is why it can be said that Mary, at one and the same time, can be identified as being betrothed to Joseph and his wife as well.

The second passage is Luke 1:26–38. In this instance, the angel Gabriel visits Mary to inform her that she is to have a baby whose birth will be the work of the Holy Spirit. These are the two passages that provide any information regarding the birth of our Lord. It is striking to note that the gospel of Mark, the first gospel to be written, makes no such reference at all. Neither does the gospel of John. Further, there is no correlative data provided in the rest of the New Testament—not by Peter, James, John, or Paul. One wonders why these writers make no mention of the birth of Jesus if the matter of the virgin birth is of ultimate importance.

We know that by the middle of the second century, the virgin birth had become a widely spread and generally accepted component of the Christian faith. Essentially, the Christian community came to affirm that Jesus Christ was a direct descendent of King David, according to the flesh, but the Son of God by divine will and word. Thus, it was from such a growing conviction that the strong creedal statements were formulated. And it is the strong creedal statements that continue to influence the worship rituals of the church even to this day.

This is not a matter about which I feel the necessity for an immovable dogmatism. I respect the inclusion of the advent narrative as found in Matthew and Luke. I am provoked to ponder the obvious absence of such reference in Mark, John, and the rest of the New Testament. Why does such perplexing diversity exist? I simply do not know. However, it does not matter to me because my faith in Jesus does not depend on the circumstance of his birth, but, rather, on the validity of his resurrection. The singular emphasis of apostolic proclamation was the death, burial, and resurrection of Jesus. Therefore, as far as I *am* concerned, the virgin birth is not in the forefront of Christian faith and doctrine. I am quite willing to allow each believer, intelligently and prayerfully, to choose his or her own interpretation. For me, the important focus is to discover, appropriate, and proclaim the truth of God as that truth is made known to us through the scriptures and by the process of special revelation.

## *He Suffered Under Pontius Pilate*
## *Was Crucified*
## *Dead and Buried*

It is quite interesting that the only human name mentioned in the Apostles' Creed is the name of the Roman governor, Pontius Pilate. We know him as the ruler who presided over the greatest crime ever perpetuated in the halls of legal jurisprudence. There is no doubt that Pilate is correctly held responsible for the ultimate decision in the trial of Jesus. Although by Roman custom regarding occupied countries, the Jewish Sanhedrin, was the effective administrative body in Judea. However, the singular limitation on the authority of the Sanhedrin was that they could not initiate or carry out the death sentence. Thus, the final verdict in this instance was in the hands of Pontius Pilate, the governor of Judea. Further, the Roman law dictated that Pilate could not delegate the responsibility of making this decision to anyone else.

Actually, I find myself feeling sympathy for Pilate, for he found himself in a very tough position. Keeping peace with the hostile and generally rebellious Jewish population certainly was no walk in the park. Indeed, all his gifts of arbitration and compromise were constantly employed to maintain some semblance of law and order within the fractious community. And the religious leaders of the Jews wanted Jesus killed because he was a powerful voice interjecting an antithetical view to their own regarding the *Torah* and will of God. Pilate knew what they wanted, and he was familiar with their methods of achieving their desires. He knew all too well the embittered hostility of the Jewish community to Rome, and he was not retaining any false delusions regarding the significance of their pious protestations of loyalty to Caesar as their true and only sovereign.

Do we have a clue regarding Pilate's attitude toward Jesus? The record shows that it was Pilate's desire to release Jesus (John 19:12). As a matter of fact, that one brief sentence summarizes the attitude of Pilate throughout the trial of Jesus: "From then on Pilate tried to release him." Jesus was unlike any criminal ever brought before him. He presented no form of defense on his own behalf; he showed no defiance or violent outbursts; he was not panic-stricken and made no plea for mercy. Rather, he was a regal and quiet man whose very presence communicated serenity.

Through the years, I have continued to find myself with increasing sympathy for Pontius Pilate. After all, he was in the grip of political and religious forces that far exceeded his mental, emotional, and physical abilities. Ultimately, his action of surrendering Jesus into the hands of the angry mob initiated an inevitable horror from which his memory cannot be extricated. In simple terms, I believe that Pilate did the wrong thing because he lacked the moral courage to do the right thing. I wonder how often in my own life I have chosen to fail my Lord because of a desire to achieve some supposed worldly ambition. At any rate, I can only say of Pilate those self-condemning words: *There, but for the grace of God, go I.*

It is inevitable that each of us must confront the question of the relevance of the passion of our Lord to ourselves. In other words, each of us must face the unavoidable question: *To what extent does the cross event impact my own life?* It seems to me that certain factors exist as essential components of the issue.

1. *The cross indicts me as a sinner.* I am told that one of the favorite hymns continues to be "The Old Rugged Cross." It seems to me that the text of the song has a way of placing the event of the cross long ago and far away: "On a hill far away stood an old rugged cross." I can sing that song with a nostalgic affection because it makes the event so very remote from me in time and circumstance. However, there is one song that forces me into the experience in a very personal way. Consider the lines of "When I Survey the Wondrous Cross:"

   When I survey the wondrous cross
   on which the Prince of Glory died,
   my richest gain I count but loss,
   and pour contempt on all my pride.

   Better yet, ponder these lines from "Amazing Grace":

   Amazing grace! How sweet the sound,
   that saved a wretch like me!
   I once was lost, but now am found;
   was blind, but now I see.

In other words, the question of the African-American spiritual summons an answer: "Were you there when they crucified my Lord?" Yes, I was there. We all were there. The cross remains an existential declaration that Jesus's death is the price of the wrath of God against our disobedience. Ultimately, it is the eternal evidence that God loves us too much to simply ignore or shrug off our sin. He takes us and our sin seriously. Couch it anyway you wish, but in the final analysis, the suffering and death of Jesus is the eternal proof that God cares for me and you! And that is the Good News of Jesus Christ. In light of all the aforementioned, I believe in Jesus Christ as God's Son and my personal Savior. Further, I know that to reject Jesus is to reject God himself.

2. *The cross is the assurance that I am a forgiven sinner.* Along with the recitation of the Apostles' Creed during our worship experiences, we often join other believers in the Lord's Prayer. At the very heart of that prayer, one finds the poignant petition: *And forgive us our debts (trespasses).* Jesus taught his disciples to seek God's forgiveness because he knew that all people are sinners. So our prayer is, "Forgive us our debts." And the cross vividly responds, "Your debts are forgiven." Surely this makes a profound impression upon us! This does not mean that I no longer am a sinner. I am and forever remain a sinner. I have been disloyal to God. By word and deed, I have offended other people. I am guilty of all that I have done and said that has broken God's perfect law and brought harm to others. The damage of my sin remains. I am a sinner! However, in the cross, and by the grace of God, I am a forgiven sinner. And that truly is the gospel!

3. *The cross is the instrument of reconciliation.* It is at this point that the full meaning of the word *atonement* emerges. What does this mean? Well, consider the word in this fashion: *at-one-ment.* The cross makes us one with God. This is reconciliation. Indeed, this is a blessed assurance. Yet it means much more. The cross makes possible a right relationship with other people as well. I have no problem with the first component, but often I have struggled with the second. I feel at peace regarding my acceptance by God. However, I frequently am bothered about my acceptance, or the lack thereof, of certain individuals and

groups of individuals. To say the least, I experience a limited reconciliation with those "suspicious" individuals or groups. I must remember at all times that the purpose of the cross is to provide total reconciliation between myself and God, and myself and *all* other people. I am assisted in this matter when I pause to read with discernment that best known text: "For God so loved the world, that he gave his only begotten Son" (John 3:16 KJV). The Christ event on the cross removes the barriers between man and God. Certainly, it removes the barriers between man and man. After all, the cross is the universal and all-encompassing instrument of reconciliation. So it is that the suffering of our Lord and the sorrow that exists in the heart of God are the price of the peace I know with God.

Then there is the matter of the emphasis on the fact that Jesus was *dead and buried*. After all these years of reflecting on and studying the life and ministry of Jesus, I still retain the personal prerogative of intellectual dialogue with the extant narrative itself. For example, believing as I do in the deity of Jesus, I wrestle with the notion that, in the crucifixion of Jesus, God himself died! That, to me, remains an amazing conclusion that defies practical reason. Perhaps that is the reason that in the New Testament itself, as well as in the classic creeds of the church, great and reiterated emphasis is given to the fact that Jesus really died. Consider the following:

> Then Jesus cried again with a loud voice and breathed his last. (Matthew 27:50 NRSV)

> Now when the centurion who stood facing him, saw that in this way he breathed his last, he said, "Truly this man was God's Son." (Mark 15:39 NRSV)

> Then Jesus, crying with a loud voice, said, "Father, into your hands I commend my spirit." Having said this, he breathed his last. When the centurion saw what had taken place, he praised God and said, "Certainly this man was innocent.' And when all the crowds who had gathered there for this spectacle saw what had taken place, they returned home, beating their breasts. But all his acquaintances, including

> the women who had followed him from Galilee, stood at
> a distance, watching these things. (Luke 23:46–49 NRSV)

I find it quite compelling to recall that in John's gospel, he tells of the spear thrust into the side of Jesus, as if to leave out no detail that contributes to Jesus's death. The earliest Christian preachers gave great emphasis to the death of Jesus. Further, they recorded in great detail his burial, indicating how his body was laid in the tomb, wrapped in grave-clothes and the shroud after it was embalmed with the perfumes used in that day in the preparation of the bodies of the dead. With great force, Peter proclaimed that grim event: "This Jesus, you crucified and killed" (Acts 2:23 NRSV). "You killed the author of life" (Acts 3:15 NRSV). I find the same conviction to have dominated the apostolic proclamations in the early church (Acts 7:52, 10:39, 13:8–9, 1 Corinthians 15:3).

As one who has embraced the validity of a measure of reverent agnosticism, eventually it becomes essential that I formulate a theological *apologia* to which I can subscribe and which I can proclaim. Therefore, the following is a rather simplistic synthesis of my evolving reflections:

1. The purpose of the incarnation was to deal with the sin of humankind. Therefore, it was essential that Jesus confront the reality of sin in inevitable ultimate conflict. Thereby, he proved that sin never could defeat his love, nor destroy his life.

2. The experience of death is the ultimate experience of the human race. As the incarnation is the reality of God's entering into the human experience, then death is the unavoidable eventuality for Jesus Christ.

3. In the cross event, the validity of Jesus Christ as victim and victor truly is confirmed. In other words, Jesus had to suffer before he could reign. Because of his victory over sin and death, the Lamb of God becomes the Lord of Glory.

## On the Third Day, He Rose Again from the Dead

We have arrived at the supremely critical component of the Christian faith. The claim that Jesus rose from the dead is so profoundly cosmic in its inferences, implications, and effects that there can be no intellectual vacillations in the matter. Plainly stated, the resurrection is either the greatest event in the human odyssey or it is the greatest lie ever perpetuated on humankind. This is the reason that none of us can afford to take a casual and noncritical approach to the subject.

It is significant to examine the attitudes and convictions pertaining to the resurrection held by those persons who were eye-witnesses to the Passion Week and its aftermath. I, for one, want to know what they experienced, what they thought, and what they said about the event. Of course, the basic text for such research is the book of Acts. Herein is recorded the sermonic content of apostolic preaching. There is an abundant evidence that belief in the resurrection was the essential foundation of the church's faith. In this regard, one may consider the sermons recorded throughout the book of Acts: 2:24–36; 3:15; 4:10; 7:56; 10:40; 13:30–37; 17:31. One fact becomes unmistakable: if the resurrection is removed from the faith expressions of the church, all other components of the Christ narrative are invalidated forthwith.

Regarding the authenticity of the resurrection of Jesus, we face one major problem: no person saw the resurrection taking place. Consider another way to state the situation: there are no witnesses to the resurrection. Then what are we dependent on to validate our common faith? We are dependent on persons who affirm that they have seen the risen Christ. There are several such accounts. Perhaps the apostle Paul has summarized them in succinct form:

> For I handed on to you as of first importance what I in turn had received: that Christ died for our sins in accordance with the scriptures, and that he was buried, and that he was raised on the third day in accordance with the scriptures, and that he appeared to Cephas, then to the twelve. Then he appeared to more than five hundred brothers and sisters at one time, most of whom are still alive though some have died. Then he appeared to James, then to all the apostles. Last of all, as one untimely born, he appeared also to me. (1 Corinthians 15:3–8 NRSV)

Surely it likely is appropriate to analyze In some depth the credibility of the witnesses of the risen Christ. And at other times and in other circumstances, I have participated in such collegiate dialogue. However, it is my purpose in this writing simply to confirm that I believe in the reality of the resurrection of Jesus from the dead. It is fitting, it seems to me, to provide some personal theological impression regarding this transcendent of all events in human history. Therefore, as directly as I can state it, here is my own view of the fact and meaning of the resurrection:

> I believe that God raised Jesus from the dead. I believe that this statement should be viewed in apocalyptic terms. This means that in the resurrection, the total psychosomatic being of Jesus was translated into a transformed eschatological existence. Thus, I mean that the resurrected Christ revealed an etheric body that was mysteriously super-physical and spiritually psychical.

> I am convinced that this resurrected personality was of such etheric texture as to be essentially malleable by transcendent thought. Further, I strongly believe that in his resurrection, Christ reveals the ultimate resurrection destiny of those who, by faith, have embraced the salvation of God in Jesus.

All of these observations have been shared so that I can justify the following declaration: This is why I believe in Jesus Christ! How important is this doctrine to me, to each believer, to the church as a whole? Clearly stated, without the resurrection, there would be no Christianity, no church, and no hope for the actualization of the promised kingdom of God. Yes, it is infinitely important! I believe it, and I believe in Jesus Christ!

### He Ascended into Heaven

In our liturgical recitations, reference to the ascension of Jesus inevitably follows the proclamation of our faith in his resurrection. As a rule, that is about all we do with this aspect of the story. We say the words, and then we move on to the next creedal statement. Small wonder! The ascension surely is the most confusing event to describe or comprehend. I have seen paintings by reputable artists that purport to provide a visual interpretation. However, I have never seen one that seemed adequate for the subject. I think that the writers of the New

Testament struggled with the incident as much as we do. They give very little time and space to their descriptions. Indeed, the ascension is the victim of profound neglect in the theological presentations of biblical scholars, preachers, and teachers.

When I join the congregation in saying those few words, "He ascended into heaven," what am I really saying? What do I really believe? Am I merely bound by the strictures of ecclesiastical tradition, or is there authentic substance to my affirmation? I shall attempt to explain my personal view on the matter. In elementary terms, I am unable to separate the events of the resurrection and the ascension. I see them as inextricably linked together. They, together, complete the story that the suffering and crucified Christ is risen and ascended into the presence and glory of God. So what does this mean? It means that the ascended Christ has taken his throne as the King of Glory. As it is recorded in Revelation 1:5, Christ is the ruler of the kings of earth.

Such thinking as this goes far toward satisfying thoughts pertaining to the meaning of the ascension for the church as a whole. Frankly, I need to think in more personal terms as well. So what does the ascension mean to me as an individual? When a believer becomes one with the Lord in faith and practice, he shares in the various experiences of the Lord. Surely that is what Paul is saying in Philippians 3:10–11 (NRSV):

> I want to know Christ and the power of his resurrection and the sharing of his sufferings by becoming like him in his death, if somehow I may attain the resurrection from the dead.

If such is the case, and I believe that it is, when my Lord is risen and exalted into glory, so will I be also! And that will be glory for me!

### And (He) Sitteth on the Right Hand of God the Father Almighty

The ascension is a fitting conclusion to the earthly life of Jesus. Practically speaking, with the ascension, Jesus disappears from this natural, mortal experience. As the ascension writes "The End" to his earthly ministry, it also writes "The Beginning" to his heavenly role as the King of Glory. The early church interpreted this as the promotion or exaltation of Jesus the Christ. Perhaps Jesus framed this understanding himself when he quoted Psalm 110:1 (NRSV): "The Lord says to my Lord, Sit at my right hand until I make your enemies your footstool" (Matthew 22:44; Mark 12:36; Luke 21:42 NRSV). This thought was dominant in Peter's sermon: "God exalted him at his right hand as Leader and Savior" (Acts 5:31 NRSV). Of course, there are other equally compelling passages, but these are enough to illustrate the point.

The creedal statement gives emphasis to the idea of Jesus Christ sitting at the right hand of God. This imagery suggests royalty, honor, and glory that is his in heaven. There is another passage with quite a different point of view. As he was facing death for his witness, Stephen makes the following memorable statement: "I see the heavens opened, and the Son of Man *standing* at the right hand of God" (Acts 7:56 NRSV). I like this passage above all others pertaining to this matter. I perceive this as a picture of the Christ as mighty and ready to respond to us in our times of struggle and suffering. In other words, in his exalted state, he remembers his own. This I believe, and this is one reason I believe in Jesus.

### From Thence He Shall Come to Judge the Quick and the Dead

With these words, we affirm two distinct doctrines of the church: (1) The Second Coming of Jesus to earth, and (2) the coming judgment of God. Generally speaking, although Christians throughout the world recite these words each Lord's Day, there are relatively few sermons preached on them anymore. Yet, here they are! What are we to make of them?

In his writings to the Christians of Thessalonica, Paul provides us with significant insight into the nature and meaning of the *parousia*, the Second Coming:

> The Lord himself,
> with a cry of command,
> with the archangel's call,
> and with the sound of God's trumpet,
> will descend from heaven.
> And the dead in Christ will rise first;
> then we (who are alive and left)

shall be caught up together with them (in
the clouds) to escort the Lord in the air.
(1 Thessalonians 4:16f NRSV)

I shall leave to others the task of parsing this text from any particular eschatological perspective appropriate to them. After all these many years of reading and listening to the varied theological interpretations pertaining to the ultimate destiny of humanity and the universe, I have become weary of the rigid positioning of the respective schools of thought. Therefore, I shall attempt a personal synthesis of the subject, realizing that the only person who may be willing to affirm such a point of view is myself. Thus, what exactly is the summary intent of the writers of the New Testament as they speak of the Second Coming and the inevitable judgment to follow?

In poetic, philosophical, and theological imagery, it is my view that the weight of the biblical revelation indicates a cosmic culmination, that is a universal moment of total redemption. By this, I mean that the ultimate intent of God is to bring into cohesive union with himself the last atom of his altogether perfect creation. Essentially, the cosmos is spiritual in nature, and, therefore, moves inexorably toward the salvation that results in absolute union with God. Certain biblical references retain intimations of such logic:

For God so loved the world. (John 3:16 NRSV)

We know that the whole creation has been groaning in labor pains until now; and not only the creation, but we ourselves, who have the first fruits of the Spirit, groan inwardly while we wait for the adoption, the redemption of our bodies. (Romans 8:22–23 NRSV)

When all things are subjected to him, then the Son himself will also be subjected to the one who put all things in subjection under him, *so that God may be all in all.* (1 Corinthians 15:28 NRSV; my emphasis)

The progressive ideas contained in these texts (and many others similar to these) retain an inherent mystery that defies simplistic analysis. The notion of putting such transcendent images into easy-to

-understand language is quite challenging. Nevertheless, it seems to me that the eschatological corpus of the biblical material draws the picture of the total transformation of the material universe into an intangible, subjective, and spiritual essence rather than a tangible (even if remote), objective, and material actuality. In other words, the biblical story suggests that the natural order of all things will be reversed, and the world as we know it will enter into a new sphere of reality.

In light of all of this, what is the scenario for us as Christians? Referring to the First Corinthians passage cited above, when Christ has consummated the process of the building of the body of Christ, he will deliver himself, with his entire completed body (the church), in a spiritual union that, at length, is prepared for entering the essential reality of God himself. Such will be the Second Coming, which initiates a universal process involving divine judgment and redemption. And in it all, each of us is capsulated into the loving embrace of God the Father Almighty, in which we all become essentially one while retaining awareness of our unique and individual selfhood.

It is acknowledged that the specific and technical details of familiar eschatological analysis and instruction are absent from this discussion. They are intended to be so. As indicated earlier, these thoughts constitute the synthesis of many years reflection. There is no claim here that these ideas constitute ultimate truth. Not by a long shot! However, these thoughts allow me to have peace in the balance between reason and faith. In the end, the poetic and apocalyptic language of Revelation 21:1–4 NRSV provides the perfect summary:

> And I saw a new heaven and a new earth; for the first heaven and the first earth had passed away, and the sea was no more. And I saw the Holy City, the new Jerusalem, coming down out of heaven from God, prepared as a bride adorned for her husband. And I heard a loud voice from the throne saying,
>
> *"See, the home of God is among mortals. He will dwell with them; they will be his peoples, and God himself will be with them; he will wipe every tear from their eyes. Death will be no more; mourning and crying and pain will be no more; for the first things have passed away."*

One of the guiding mentors in my lifelong quest for intellectual and spiritual balance has been St. Augustine. Pertaining to the discussing of the finality of the human odyssey and the anticipated eternal future before us, the summary observation by Augustine has been an abiding inspiration for me:

> And that seventh age will be our Sabbath, a day that knows no evening, but is followed by the Day of the Lord, an everlasting eighth day, hallowed by the resurrection of Christ, prefiguring the eternal rest not only of the spirit, but of the body as well. Then we shall have holiday and we shall see, we shall see and we shall love, we shall love and we shall praise. Behold, this is how it shall be at the end without end. For what else is our end, but to come to that Kingdom which has no end. (*De civitate Dei*, 22.30)

# WHY I BELIEVE IN THE HOLY SPIRIT

[I believe in] the Holy Spirit.
—The Apostles' Creed

For a good part of my life, I have wrestled with the Christian doctrine of the Holy Spirit. From my earliest days, words always have had meaning for me. In those formative years, it was quite customary to hear people speak of the Holy Ghost rather than the Holy Spirit. The notion of *ghost* became a confusing issue for me. On one hand, it communicated images of a mysterious specter gliding about the mental environs of my thought processes. There were those mischievous Halloween ghost types that annually occupied center stage for a brief season. Then there were the reports of the ghosts of the departed who populated haunted houses and frightened residents and visitors alike. How, therefore, does a young and inquisitive mind make an untroubled transition to the idea of some Holy Ghost who merits adoration and worship?

In due time, the language of the liturgies and worship expressions evolved, and the use of *Holy Spirit* replaced the older term, *Holy Ghost.* That, in my judgment, is a very good thing! At least, one now can identify, with increased clarity, the biblical intent pertaining to this admittedly challenging component of Christian doctrine. Although this remains, for me, the most obtuse aspect of our common faith, I, nevertheless, am provided a bridge to the exercise of reason and faith in this regard.

Speaking of reason, when the discussion pertains to the Holy Spirit, I am not out of the woods yet. The creeds of the church affirm a belief in the Father, Son, and Holy Spirit. This is called *the doctrine of the Trinity.* What does this mean? Simply stated, God is three in one, and one in three. Unless one accepts this declaration without judicious analysis, he may discover himself captured between two dangerous concepts. From one perspective, there exists the possibility of *tritheism,* resulting in Father, Son, and Holy Spirit being three distinct deities (a sort of sacred *Troika*). In contrast, there is *Unitarianism,* in which the Father is God alone, and the Son is relegated to the status of simply being a singularly great person, and the Holy Spirit becomes little more than impersonal energy or power force influencing, by subjective impulse, the thinking and action of individuals.

As it is likely true of most believers, the time arrived in my own faith pilgrimage when it became necessary that I seek to identify for myself the divine purpose in the person, nature, and mission of the Holy Spirit. Such proved to be of no small consequence. Of course, I found myself returning again to the primary source book regarding the Holy Spirit— that is, the book of Acts in our New Testament. By the time I reached the second chapter of Acts, I was convinced that the Holy Spirit was the central reality of the faith of those first Christians. Further, I discovered that in the early church, the Holy Spirit did not appear as a component of creedal conviction and instructional doctrine. Rather, the Holy Spirit was personal, vital, and a consistently powerful existential experience. It is my observation that the contribution of the Holy Spirit to the apostolic church was characterized by intimacy and power. In reflection, I see no indication that such characterization ever would be altered by time or circumstance. In other words, true to the character of God himself, the Holy Spirit remains the same yesterday, today, and forever.

In the earlier years of my ministry, there was a *neo-Pentecostal* movement that swept through the Christian community, including all Christian bodies from Roman Catholics, the mainline Protestant churches, and the Pentecostal denominations as well. This phenomenon was known as the *charismatic movement.* While, for the most part, it proved to be spiritually beneficial to those who were involved, there were many instances of conflict as well. In retrospect, although I felt a keen interest in the process, I was never drawn into a personal commitment to either school of thought. In other words, this was never an issue of primary significance to me. Therefore, the moment came when I was moved to articulate for myself a position that retained a balanced perspective. Simply stated, that perspective is as follows:

1. The Holy Spirit is, in essence, God.
2. The word *incarnation* provides the key to understanding the nature and work of the Holy Spirit.
3. As God was in Jesus Christ as the divine incarnation in human life, so God is incarnate in the Holy Spirit as divine power in our midst.
4. Thinking of the Holy Spirit is the tangible way of describing what God *does*.
5. Finally, the idea of the Holy Spirit is one way to speak of the activity of God on earth accomplishing his will and works.

Surely it is to Jesus, our Lord, that one turns for the ultimately relevant answer to the question, "Who is the Holy Spirit?" Jesus answers:

> It is to your advantage that I go away, for if I do not go away, the Counselor will not come to you; but If I go, I will send him to you. And when he comes, he will convince the world concerning sin and righteousness and judgment … When the Spirit of truth comes, he will guide you into all truth. (John 16:7–8, 13 NRSV)

It seems to me that Jesus's promise is that the continuing and constant presence of God himself is assured. Surely this is a promise that should generate great joy among all Christians. Some of us Christians act as if we are afraid of the Holy Spirit. We disdain the thought of being identified as some Holy Joe or a Holy roller. Perhaps, in this age of the objective and the tangible, we have surrendered our confidence in the supernatural, forgetting that the foundation of the supernatural is the Holy Spirit.

With the passing of the years, I have become convinced that if I remain familiar with the forms of religion, but lack the spiritual energy bestowed by the existential experience of the indwelling Holy Spirit, I am an empty religious shell, devoid of the capacity to accomplish Christ's mission for my life. Therefore, for me, the Holy Spirit is the divine reality of personal and collective Christian apprehension and remains of ultimate importance for my daily and developing needs. This, I think, is true of all Christians.

# WHY I BELIEVE IN THE HOLY CATHOLIC (UNIVERSAL) CHURCH

> [I believe in] the Holy Catholic [Universal] Church.
> —The Apostles' Creed

In discussing the church, I like the longer statement of the Nicene Creed: "I believe in the one, holy, Catholic and apostolic church." In this longer statement, the complete nature of the church is identified. Reference is made to the unity of the church. It is declared to be one entity. Its life is in the one God who creates one people from all people from all places and all ages. On this basis, I affirm the principle of ecumenicity.

Further, it speaks of the holy church. It is holy because God is present in, with, through, and for the church. God ensures that there will always be the church, and it will always be holy.

Reference to the catholicity of the church is a positive declaration that the church transcends provincialism and sectarian bias. It speaks of the whole church, the complete body of Christ, and the entire people of God. (This is a grand statement, and I pray to God that someday it may be actualized.)

The idea of the *apostolicity* of the church has great significance. It asserts that the church remains the custodian of the keys of the kingdom as given to the apostles (Matthew 16:19). In other words, the divine mission as given by Jesus abides with the church until the end of time. (I like this because it means that the Christian has great job security! Always, we have a task to accomplish for the Lord!)

In a significant way, this declaration answers the question, "What is the true church?" Although this discussion is intended to confirm the familiar statement in the Apostles' Creed, remember that we are developing the content of the less familiar Nicene Creed. This has remained the constant dogma of the church since the Council of Constantinople in 381 A.D. Apart from its ecclesiastical and historical importance, this version of the creedal statement has very special significance for me.

In 1992, Jeanette and I were visiting on the campus of Boston College. The occasion was the convocation of a National Catholic Ecumenical Dialogue. We were invited by Fr. Thomas Groome of the university faculty to attend a special evening service. Gladly, we accepted his gracious invitation. As far as we were aware, we were the only Protestants present. This was a moment of supreme importance for Jeanette and me for two reasons: (1) We had become disillusioned by the rigid and unbending fundamentalist posture of the prevailing Baptist mentality, our lifelong denominational affiliation; (2) The speaker of the evening was to be the esteemed Rev. Dr. Raymond Brown, professor of New Testament in the Union Theological Seminary of New York.

We sat in the vast audience, listening to one of the great intellects of the Christian world. He was speaking on the true nature of the New Testament church. To the best of my ability, I was attempting to follow his discussion (including his frequent use of Latin phrases, which I struggled to comprehend). At one point in his address, he quoted in Greek a phrase that I immediately understood. Quickly, I wrote that phrase down on an envelope I found in the back of the seat in front of me. It seemed to be God's personal word for me that night:

*I believe in one, holy, Catholic, and apostolic church.*

The long-held concepts of the denominational restraints that had been a delimiting factor in my personal spiritual growth began to melt away. The provincialism, prejudice, and traditionalism were diminished in the brilliant light of true revelation. One might say that I truly was born again that night. I began to grasp something of God's intent for his church. It has been almost a quarter century since that mind- and life-changing event in the chapel of Boston college. I have grown to think of the church in two dimensions: the *essential* church and the *actual* church. I realize that this distinction may sound a bit Platonic, and certainly I am influenced by the great philosopher's understanding of reality.

When I reflect on the Nicene declaration, "(I believe) in one, holy, Catholic and apostolic church," I realize that I am affirming the reality of the essential church of divine intent. To this, I can only respond that truly I regret that such an entity does not exist in real time. But what does exist in real time is the actual church, and there is absent from it any semblance of theological or organizational unity. In many ways, this visible manifestation of the body of Christ is all-too-often at war with itself. How can an entity be identified as holy when it is divided by envy, competitiveness, and closely guarded turfs of ecclesiastical power? So, the ideal of a Catholic or universal church is nullified. Indeed, the sacred robe of the Christ is rent asunder. The result is a general inability to achieve the objective of the apostolic commission and mission.

Subsequently, I am drawn to raise the issue of *relevance.* After many years of ministry in respective denominational structures, and after observing that the influence, size, and attractiveness of the visible church is in decline, I find myself confronting the relative relevance of the contemporary church. This is an issue that has summoned observations by countless specialists in the field of church growth.

Some suggest that if the church is to be relevant to the present socio political situation, it must develop the capacity to become *adaptable.* This observation sounds quite intelligent at first glance. However, I have a problem with the idea. Such a flexible and adaptable attitude allows for the possible embracing of non-spiritual elements that threaten the moral and ethical fiber of society. So, I find myself pondering the idea of becoming tolerant toward anti-God ideas and movements all in the spirit of relating to the "real world" as it is today. And what is the advice of St. Paul in this regard? Well, he does not hesitate, as you are certain to observe in Romans 12:2 (NRSV): "Do not be conformed to this world, but be transformed by the renewing of your minds, so that you may discern what is the will of God what is good and acceptable and perfect."

On the other hand, there are equally sincere people who insist that the important thing for the church is to preserve, with conviction, the time-honored traditions of the church. Quite apart from the affirming of the historical theological dogmas of the church, it is good if we do not rock the boat. After all, it is better to be safe than sorry! To say the least, such action is far less disruptive than getting involved with "all this change."

Frankly, I reject both of these approaches. Why? Well, on one hand, the principle of adaptation has the potential of succumbing to modernism for the pure sake of reflecting that which is socially or politically correct. On the other hand, forever looking back to the faith of our fathers as the gold standard for "doing church" is to embrace pure traditionalism. In my judgment, either approach can be idolatrous in practice and consequence.

So, what about the notion of relevance? How can the church be relevant in this society—or any other society? When is the church relevant? At this point, I feel very strongly that the church is relevant in this or any society, in this or any age, when the gospel of Jesus Christ is the guiding criterion (not the traditions of the past, and not the fads and fancies of the present). The gospel is relevant as proclaimed by Jesus himself and to which the apostles bore witness. In other words, the message of Jesus Christ, as affirmed by the apostles, is the singular and altogether adequate guide for the church of this age or any age.

I am not a prophet. Neither am I the son of a prophet. However, I strongly believe that it is the divine intent of God for his church to be one! That golden idea and ideal can only be achieved when all sects, denominations, and ecclesiastical systems of all kinds will consent to the principle regarding the gospel of Jesus Christ, as given by Jesus himself and affirmed by the apostles, as the only and singular guiding criterion. Then, and only then, can the seamless robe of our Lord be restored.

> I have other sheep ... I must bring them also, and they will listen to my voice. So there will be one flock, one shepherd. (John 10:16 NRSV)

# WHY I BELIEVE IN THE COMMUNION OF SAINTS

[I believe in] the communion of saints.
—The Apostles' Creed

This affirmation becomes increasingly significant to me with the passing of the years. Again, as I reflect on the use of the words involved, their meaning is greatly intensified. The two key words involved here are *koinonia* and *hagion* ("communion" and "saints"). It strikes me as an article of unusual interest because it differs from the other articles of our common creed. This article gives importance to an experience of the community of faith rather than an object of faith.

The word *koinonia* is not exclusive to the New Testament or the creedal statements of the Christian community. Long before the birth of the church, this word was common to the vocabulary of the great Greek philosophers and writers. If we are to comprehend the understanding of the church regarding the word, we should be aware of its use throughout the Greek-speaking world. It was employed by the Greeks to describe any relationship, partnership, fellowship, activity, or experience that brought people together. Hence, the root meaning of the word is "togetherness."

In his *Politics* (1334–33 BC), Aristotle speaks of marriage as a *koinonia.* In the Greek marriage contract, two people take each other for partnership, fellowship, and to share all of life. *Koinonia* was used to describe a business relationship, partnership in education, and the social life within the community. It was also employed to affirm a fellowship with a deity. In light of all of the aforementioned, those early believers were conscious of the broad implications inherent in their use of *koinonia*. Therefore, we should understand that this confession article means that Christians live in mutual care, love, and sharing with each other.

The word *hagion* amplifies and enlarges the scope of the *koinonia*. It is appropriate to consider who the saints are who are mentioned in this creedal statement. I suppose that I could take the time to list or provide the written texts of the many references to the saints who may be found in the scriptures. However, the purpose of this effort is to share my personal thoughts regarding these creedal tenets. Perhaps the thoughts of the great musical theologian Charles Wesley can provide an insight to my own view regarding our communion with the saints:

> One family we dwell in him,
> One Church, above, beneath,
> Though now divided by the stream,
> The narrow stream of death.

There, in beautiful, poetic expression, is the effective summary of my own personal reflections. Nevertheless, I shall share, with simpler language, my thoughts. I believe that the communion of the saints refers to the fellowship available to all believers with the Father, Son, and Holy Spirit. Further, I am sensitive to the reality of the bond that binds me to all other believers (saints) in Christ who presently live in this world. And that fellowship bond is inclusive of all people of all ages, of all races, from all places. Indeed, no believer in God, through Jesus Christ, is excluded from the loving tether of Christian communion. Further, I am convinced that the communion of saints includes all those who have entered into eternal life in the presence of God. Surely, this was the intent of the writer of Hebrews as he spoke to this issue (12:1 NRSV): "Therefore, since we are surrounded by so great a cloud of witnesses, let us also lay aside every weight and the sin that clings so closely."

The singular basis for communion between Christians is Jesus Christ, and that basis cannot be abrogated by death. If, indeed, we can have fellowship with our risen Lord (who died for us), we can have fellowship with those who died in Christ. The older I get, the more I understand the blessedness of fellowship with that "great cloud of witnesses" mentioned above. So, where does such thinking leave us? It leaves us confident that we share in an intimate union with all members of the body of Christ, those whom we see in church next Sunday, and those whom we shall see in heaven shortly.

# WHY I BELIEVE IN THE FORGIVENESS OF SINS

[I believe in] the forgiveness of sins.
—The Apostles' Creed

Initially, this article of the Apostles' Creed suggests to me a provocative contrast between what many of the self-righteous church attendees think of themselves and what they are affirming their personal and collective need to be. In other words, we tend to mouth these words with a certain bloated piety, assuming that if we do need forgiveness for our sins, we do not need much. After all, as people and conduct and morality and ethics go, we tend to be rather normally good people. Thus, it becomes a somewhat perfunctory recitation when we utter those generic words: "I believe in the forgiveness of sins."

Perhaps our perception of the nature of forgiveness is somewhat distorted. Is it likely that when we consider the matter of forgiveness of sins, we are thinking horizontally rather than vertically? What have I said or done injurious to my spouse, my friend, my neighbor, or even my enemy? In what way have I sinned against society? Am I guilty of the sin of prejudice against a person or a group? Do I share in the collective social and national guilt of genocide against the native Americans during the eighteenth and nineteenth centuries in this country? And what about the collective social guilt pertaining to the institution of slavery? Do I find myself culpable regarding any one or more of the stated issues? If so, how do I proceed to absolve myself of any sense of guilt in the matter? Do I feel the need for any measure of forgiveness for my personal failure (sin)? If, indeed, I "believe in the forgiveness of sins," do I really believe that any one of the suggested victims of my sin actually will forgive me?

Frankly, I think that it is most unlikely that any one of the aforementioned victims is likely to extend to me any measure of unconditional forgiveness. If this is true, then I shall never experience the liberating freedom of a genuinely forgiven spirit. I am doomed to live with my guilt in perpetuity. However, suppose we are able to consider the experience of forgiveness from a vertical perspective. This is a good point for us to allow the scriptures to set the table for us:

> For I know my transgressions,
>     and my sin is ever before me.
> Against you, you alone, have I sinned,
>     and done what is evil in your sight,
> So that you are justified in your sentence
>     and blameless when you pass judgment.
> Indeed, I was born guilty,
>     a sinner when my mother conceived me. (Psalm 51:3–5 NRSV)

It is good to remember that these words, attributed to King David, are written by one who has committed adultery with Bathsheba and then arranged for the murder of her husband. This is a remarkable passage in that it enables us to realize that all sin is a sin against God. What are the spiritual and psychological benefits of this redemptive principle? Simply stated, if I have sought and received forgiveness from God for any perceived sin against any individual or group, I can live at peace, even if the offended individual or group remains unable or unwilling to forgive me. The ideal, of course, is to seek and achieve forgiveness on both the horizontal and vertical plains. It is good to know that God is forever willing to forgive. It is regretful to know that often we human beings are unwilling. In any instance, the spiritually mature person accepts the given, assimilates the therapeutic benefits into his or her personal psyche, and designs a continuing pattern of positive progression into the future.

I have thought about this matter often. After all, it has been essential for my own spiritual odyssey to honestly face my personal weaknesses, failures, and abuses of significant persons and responsibilities. Therefore, I have often reflected on the best possible procedure for myself if, indeed, I *am* to realize the benefits inherent in the forgiveness experience. So, it seems increasingly plausible to me to affirm as personally relevant the following steps:

1. Humbly attempt to allow the offended one (victim?) the opportunity to be a forgiving person. Admittedly, this never can be a forced arrangement, but the effort is essential to the psychological and spiritual redemptive process.

2. Humbly seek the saving response of a forgiving God, remembering that all offenses (sins) are essentially an offense (sin) against God himself. There can be no physical, mental, or spiritual healing apart from the forgiveness of God.

3. Basic to all spiritual and psychological recovery, the forgiveness of self is an absolute requirement and a primary objective for us. We live in a highly therapeutic culture; therefore, there exists a natural emphasis on the process of the "getting it off the chest" confessional experience. This, in my judgment is required if one is to realize personal catharsis and psychological well-being. I refer to this as the achievement of an integrated personality.

After all this discussion, I remain pleased that we persist in using the Apostles' Creed (and especially this article on forgiveness) in our Sunday services of worship. I keep remembering that Jesus surrendered to Peter and the other apostles the keys to the kingdom. Thus, the important issue of personal and collective sin forever remains central in the sacred ministries of the church. After all, it is there, in the proclamation of the Word and observance of the sacraments, that sinful ministers are empowered to say to repentant sinners, on behalf of a forgiving God, "Go in peace. Your sins are forgiven."

This prompts one final observation regarding forgiveness. I find myself thinking of Jesus at this point. What was the central purpose of his coming in the first place? Why did he endure the shame and suffering of the cross? Why did he have to die for us? It seems to me that the answer is quite evident. Jesus did not come to earth in order to convince God, by his sacrifice on the cross, to forgive us. Rather, he came to tell us that God, in his abundant and gracious love, has forgiven us! Not only do I accept Jesus Christ, by faith, as my Savior, I also accept, by grateful faith, his forgiveness as well. In other words, *I believe in the forgiveness of sins.*

# WHY I BELIEVE IN THE RESURRECTION OF THE BODY

[I believe in] the resurrection of the body.
—The Apostles' Creed

This article, it seems to me, exists as a promise to believers that the end of life is not the end of life at all. It should be noted that the Christian religion is a religion of expectation. Always, there is for us the "Rapture of the Forward Look" (to borrow the phrase of Bishop Arthur Moore given in a lecture at Columbia Theological Seminary in 1955). Since the role of promise in the faith process is so important, it will be well to reflect on its true meaning.

Essentially, a promise is the affirmation of an approaching event that does not as yet exist. Thus, we Christians forever anticipate a future in which the promise will, in certitude, become actuality. Here, the remarks of Jesus come to mind: "If I go and prepare a place for you, I will come again and take you to myself so that where I am there you may be also" (John 14:3 NRSV). That is a promise!

Such thinking binds us to the future and creates in us a sense that the future is, in reality, history. Accordingly, when we gather to affirm collectively our faith in the resurrection of the body, we are, in essence, pausing to remember the future. At this stage in my life, I find myself often remembering the future, and I really like what I am remembering.

I must remind myself constantly that I am dealing with the subjective essence of reality and not with the actual situations of the real world. Thus, the promise exists in sharp distinction from the reality of personal experience. Therefore, it is not surprising that I find myself doubting and questioning the validity of the promise. Frankly, I am one who needs the assurance of someone in whom I have absolute trust. Fortunately for me, I have such a person. Again, listen to the assuring word of Jesus: "If this were not so, would I have told you that I go to prepare a place for you?" (John 14:2 NRSV). This is a promise!

Nevertheless, we Christians live in the tension between the Word and the redeeming of the promise. So how do we do it? How do we accomplish the continuity of our daily living in the actual world and our anticipation of living in the world to come? In very succinct fashion, Paul answers the question: "For we walk by faith, not by sight" (2 Corinthians 5:7 NRSV).

As indicated earlier, I find myself pondering these matters often these days. I suppose that I have arrived at a tentative conclusion. It is tentative because I believe that as time passes, the Spirit will guide my thinking into clearer impressions. But for now, I am at peace with the following observations: When the creed speaks of the resurrection of the body, I think reference is made to the survival of the individual personality. God does not intend that we shall be obliterated into nothing, but after death, I shall still be me, and you will still be you. What other approach complies to logic when speaking of mortal flesh that disintegrates into the original dust from which each of us originates? This is the reason that I can affirm with confidence, and in light of the knowledge now available to me, that I believe in the survival of the individual personality.

# WHY I BELIEVE IN THE LIFE EVERLASTING

And in the life everlasting.
—The Apostles' Creed

The great creedal statement concludes with the affirmation of a concept that has dominated the reflections of humankind throughout human history. From the oldest book of our canon, there comes the provocative query of Job (14:14 NRSV): "If a man die, shall he live again?" The ultimate Christian *apologia* is the clarion affirmation that everlasting life is the certain experience awaiting each of us.

The doctrine of everlasting life seems to be a bit confounding to many scholars and learned teachers of philosophy and religion. I am intrigued to recall that while, as an adult "thinking" minister, I often contemplate the complexities of such a dogma. As a child sitting at my grandmother's knee, I had no difficulty at all understanding what she meant when she said, "Charles, you will live forever." Sometimes I fortify my drift toward skepticism by recalling a strophe by Henry Wadsworth Longfellow that I was required to memorize in a high school literature class:

> Life is real! Life is earnest!
> And the grave is not its goal;
> Dust thou art, to dust returnest,
> Was not spoken of the soul.

Of course, for me, there exists that supreme declaration upon which I bet my life now and forever: *For God so loved the world, that he gave his only Son, that whoever believes in him should not perish but have everlasting life* (John 3:16; personal translation). There are many additional passages that speak of life beyond life, and each of them, I suppose, provides some measure of insight for us. However, I, for one, wish that Jesus and the apostles had been a bit more explicit in their discussion of eternal life. Of course, the apostles had not entered into that life after life as yet. But we all believe that Jesus surely had greater knowledge of the transcendent heavenly life than is recorded in the gospels. Often I have wondered why he did not share more with us in this regard. Perhaps heaven and the everlasting life are truly so utterly wonderful that full knowledge of it would motivate many of us to find ways of ending this present life just to get there.

The extant descriptions Jesus did leave us must satisfy our curiosity and insatiable appetite for more knowledge. We are left with a few hints of the glories of eternal life. Take, for instance, Jesus's beautiful portrait of heaven as given in John 14 NRSV: "In my Father's house are many rooms; if it were not so, would I have told you that I go to prepare a place for you?" The image of "Father's house" suggests many desirable and appreciated benefits, such as security, provision, fellowship, and unconditional love.

Even as I make the list of expected benefits, it comes to me that if these are the characteristics of everlasting life, then we do not have to die to experience them. Actually, we can share in the security, provision, fellowship, and unconditional love of God in the here and now! Within this present environment, we can realize a relationship with the Father, which really is the fore-winds of the coming kingdom. In other words, in the present moment, we can participate in that life which is the life of God, hence eternal life.

There is no effort here to recite an extensive component of systematic theology regarding everlasting life. Rather, it is my purpose to state with simplistic faith my personal conviction that I believe in everlasting life. There remains much about the subject that we never shall know in this life. However, we can rejoice as we enter now into that eternal relationship with the Father, knowing full well that ultimate realization of that glorious experience is beyond our greatest dreams. With Paul, I can only say, "Now we see through a mirror dimly, but then face to face. Now I know in part; then I shall understand fully, even so I have been fully understood" (1 Corinthians 13:12 NRSV).

# PART 3

## The Words of Our Religion:

## INTERPRETATIVE EXPLANATIONS OF WORDS USED IN WORSHIP AND RELIGIOUS TEACHING

# THE WORDS of OUR RELIGION

*What does that word mean?*

I have heard that question raised many times over the years. In reflection, it is apparent that we frequently employ words and terms in our corporate worship and teaching experiences without providing adequate explanation or interpretation. It is as if there exists an assumption that everybody knows the meaning of our discussion.

This section of the book is an attempt to provide some light to some of the words one frequently hears in Sunday sermons, Sunday school lessons, and certain Bible studies. Of course, the list of words included does not exhaust the words of our religious glossary. Nor does it provide an exhaustive definition of the respective words. It is, however, the hope of the author that sufficient light may be cast so that a better understanding of the content of our personal and collective faith may be achieved.

In many ways, the biblical story is made intelligible by the language we choose to use. Thus, we are possessed of a "sacred language." The language of the Christian religion is a sublime gift of God's grace. It is appropriate, therefore, that we reverently embrace it, humbly utilize it in the best possible manner, and give serious effort to comprehend its deeper meaning. Why is this important? Simply stated, it is with this sacred language that we bear witness to the grace of God through Jesus Christ, our Lord.

# ATONEMENT

*Atonement* is one of those words that suggests some sort of complicated activity by God on behalf of doomed, destitute, and depraved human beings. Since you and I are human beings, then *atonement* involves us, in some fashion. Perhaps we are not as clear in our understanding of this process as we might wish. I suppose that our uncertainty is related in some way to our being *doomed, destitute, and depraved human beings.* You might find yourself wondering where I found such a description of us. Well, actually, it goes back a very long way.

When I was a boy growing up in Atlanta, our church observed once or twice each year what was known as a *revival.* The word *revival* implies a renewal or awakening within the membership. However, in those days, *revival* actually served as a vehicle to scare sin and the devil out of young boys like me. It was then, in those *old-fashioned revival* times, that it was hammered into my young mind that I was *doomed, destitute, and depraved.* At the time, I did not understand fully what all those words meant. I only knew that they meant something very bad. Further, I was given to understand that if I failed to do something about my *lost condition,* it was certain that I would fall into a burning hell about a split second after I died. This approach created a profound problem for me. How in the world could a loving God and a loving Jesus toss an unsuspecting boy into a burning hell when he didn't even understand the meaning of the words *doomed, destitute, and depraved?* That kind of evangelism still bothers me to this very day.

The word *atonement* is a positive word. It is a good word. In simple terms, it means that God fixes whatever is wrong in our lives and in our relationship with him. Do you want it stated a bit more technically? Well try this on for size: *atonement* means "to be at one with God."

That precisely is the original meaning of the word. *Atonement* originally meant "at onement" or "reconciliation." Finally, the sensibility of that struggling young boy was alerted to the fact that God loved him so much that he freely and gladly fixed that which was wrong in his life. It was later, much later, that the boy came to understand that the simple process of God's loving gift of Jesus as his Savior was called *atonement*.

The sacred scriptures and Christian doctrine are accustomed to utilizing many words, images, and symbols to identify and explain atonement. You are familiar with those words, images, and symbols, but it will be helpful to look at them again: *sacrifice, Lamb of God, ransom, redemption, reconciliation, propitiation,* and *expiation.* It is likely that a full discussion of each of these words would prove instructive. However, is such really necessary? After all, have we not discovered the essential meaning of the word *atonement*? Is our definition not altogether sufficient? Here it is, one last time: *Atonement* means "to be at one with God because God fixes that which is wrong in our lives and in our relationship with him." Indeed, *atonement* is a positive word. It is a good word. Even a scared young boy finds that his fears are removed with such redemptive good news! Say! Atonement is good news when the young boy becomes an older man! Really, it is a word that gives me great joy!

# BAPTISM

*Baptism!* Here is one of those words that divides Christians into separate (and sometimes warring) camps. On one hand, the dunkers insist that the only valid form (another word for *technique)* of baptism is dunking, most often identified as immersion. On the other hand, there are the sprinklers, who are quite certain that less water is as efficacious as much water in its biblical and theological emphasis. Is either view to be accepted as the final word? Or, to state it differently, what does the word itself really mean?

Candidly, we must remember that the rite of baptism does not originate in the New Testament. Actually, references to sacral baths are found in the Bacchic consecrations, in the religions of ancient Egypt, the specific worship of Isis outside Egypt, in the Mithras mysteries, in the Apollinarian games, and in the festival of Pelusium. As a matter of fact, the Ganges and Euphrates came to have a religious significance comparable with that of the Jordan among Jews and Christians.

Christians usually affirm the origin of the familiar sacrament or ordinance of baptism as being the baptism of Jesus by John in the Jordan River (Mark 1:9ff). There is no doubt that baptism was practiced from the very first in the Christian community (Acts 2:38, 41; 8:12, etc.). It seems clear that the apostles understood that the existence of a missionary directive by the risen Lord involved the command to baptize. Further, from the very beginning, a distinctive formula of Christian baptism involves the inclusion of the name of Christ (Jesus). It is appropriate, I think, to ask the question, "What does baptism really mean?" Ultimately, *the significance of baptism is that it involves the intervention of the Holy God on behalf of sinful humanity.* Therefore, it is more than mere symbolism. It is proclamation. It is affirmation. It is dramatic gospel.

The act of baptism involves getting dunked or sprinkled. These words refer to technique. Theologically, technique is irrelevant. What technique communicates has pertinence. For example, dunking speaks of the end of the old life of sin. Rising from the water speaks of that new, strange, and hopeful life given by the relationship of the believer to Christ. Sprinkling provides visual attestation of the outpouring of the Holy Spirit upon the believer who is indeed "born of the Spirit" (John 3:8 NRSV).

So, what do we really have when we share in the worship ritual we call baptism? We have an experience in which God's Word comes to us in the all-too -human involvement of ministers and parishioners. In the process, God calls, renews, forgives, nourishes, and helps us through that very common commodity known as water. And what about technique (dunking and sprinkling)? Frankly, it seems to me absurd to think that either technique retains redemptive value. After all, neither a few drops of water nor a whole flowing river can ever do what only God can do: wash away our sins and make of us new creatures in Christ.

# THE BIBLE

What is there about the Bible that makes it such a special book for most people? Certainly, we realize that it has remained the central focus of the Judeo-Christian tradition through these many centuries. What is the secret of its attraction for so many of us?

Perhaps our best approach to understanding the role and influence of the Bible is to determine its singular purpose in the historic process. Generally speaking, most Christians will affirm that scripture is *given by the inspiration of God to be the rule of faith and life.* Note that I said that most of us would affirm such a statement. Frankly, I wonder how honest we are in such an affirmation. It seems to me that much of today's religious dialogue and ecclesiastical doctrinal formulations are the result of sociological and political trends and pressures. The church in our time will be well-served by an authentic renewal of biblical theology as the essential basis for doctrinal faith and social action.

If our common affirmation regarding the purpose of the Bible has any measure of relevance for us, how are we to read and understand it? Are we to take each statement, each word, each phrase, literally? I think that there is a right way to read and study the Bible, and there is a wrong way as well. The Bible is correctly read when we seek to discover who God is and how we are to live and serve faithfully in his presence. We actually render the Bible a disservice when we look to it as a scientific textbook or an accurate chronicle of world history. In fact, it is neither! Therefore, we must be prepared to encounter within the sacred pages a prescientific or even an unscientific worldview of human origins and history. We are correct in our reading of the Bible when we realize that it deals reverently with the ultimate origin and destiny of human life, which certainly transcends the scope of technical science and historical analysis.

So, what do we have in that book we call the Bible? At this point, I cannot resist a personal apologia: *In the Bible, God has spoken.* Accordingly, 2 Timothy 3:16 NRSV declares with clarity my own conviction: "All Scripture is given by inspiration of God, and is profitable for doctrine, for reproof, for correction, for instruction in righteousness." The words, "given by inspiration of God," are one compound word in the Greek that means literally "God-breathed." In other words, God so moved upon the writers of the sacred scriptures that their books are also his books. Thus, it may be stated that, as Christians, *our book,* the Bible, is essentially God's book. God grant that it ever shall remain the foundation for our faith and life.

# CHRISTIAN

This is one word that is familiar to all of us. Surely, we know and understand its meaning and significance. It is profitable, nevertheless, for us to remember that the word *Christian* was originally a pagan designation used by persons who were not believers to describe believers in Jesus. Actually, it is found only three times in the New Testament:

> And in Antioch the disciples were for the first time called Christians. (Acts 11:26 NRSV)

> In a short time you think to make me a Christian! (Acts 26:28 NRSV)

> Yet if one suffers as a Christian, let him not be ashamed, but under that name let him glorify God. (1 Peter 4:16 NRSV)

At first glance, an interesting syntax notation may be made. The word *Christian* is never employed in the New Testament as an adjective. Thus, one never finds in the Bible such expressions as "doing a Christian deed," "speaking a Christian word," or even "living a Christian life." What are we to make of this observation? Simply stated, in the New Testament, the word *Christian* refers to who one is rather than what one does.

The essential lesson to be derived from such an understanding is that before there can be a *Christian way of life,* there first must be a *Christian.* The advice we often hear (perhaps we give it ourselves) that some person should *act like a Christian* sounds so spiritual. Yet it is totally unrelated to reality unless the object of our advice is already a Christian . In other words, an individual will mature in the Lord, in faith, and in understanding after becoming a Christian. Then, it follows logically, the Christian will begin acting like a Christian.

The counsel that Jesus gave to Nicodemus remains valid. Entering the kingdom of God does not depend on what we do to inherit eternal life. Rather, it depends on our being *born again from above.* So, the Christian is that person who truly is a child of God by spiritual birth as a result of faith in the redemptive death and resurrection of Jesus of Nazareth. That is *who* the Christian *is.*

# CHURCH

One might assume that a study of the word *church* would be a simple and elemental process. After all, does not everybody know what the church is? Actually, it is not that simple and elemental. Just say the word *church* to virtually any person or group, and diverse images come to mind. After all, most of us think of some building in which we met to worship as children. Others immediately identify the word with the facility in which we meet for worship and other religious activities now. It is appropriate, therefore, that we start at the very beginning.

The Greek word used in the New Testament for *church* means "called out." To state it differently, the church is the community of people called out of the world, called together to experience God's saving and renewing grace and forgiveness, and subsequently sent back into the world from which it has been called to become agents of God's grace and forgiveness to all people. This *called-out community* is in possession of certain defining characteristics.

*We are the church.* The New Testament church is not a denomination. It is not a board, commission, or agency. It does not have a headquarters in some great American (or English or Italian) city. The church is us. We are the church. It exists whenever and wherever a group of Christians assemble in the name of Jesus Christ.

*The church is the community of the resurrection. As such, it is never to be conceived as some building.* One might wonder, in light of such thinking, why we continue to give so much time, energy, and money to the erection and maintenance of our ecclesiastical structures. Do we do this to serve God and our fellow human beings, or do we do it to serve ourselves? In other words, why do we allow our manmade structures to retain such dominance in our thinking? It is quite interesting to note that in the book of Revelation, it is pointed out that there is to be no temple in the New Jerusalem. Heaven becomes somewhat more appealing to most us when we learn that we shall not be involved in some eternal church service somewhere in the celestial realms. God knows that we have already sat through some so-called worship services that seemed like an eternity!

*God is both the architect and ruler of the church.* The composition of the church is not formed of eager volunteers who decided to assemble, organize, strategize, and actualize their own agenda. Indeed, it is God who calls out and calls together the people of his choice. It is God who continues to designate priorities, identify objectives, and specify procedures. Therefore, we are in error to speak of *our church.* In reality, if the church truly is the church, it is in every way *God's church.*

Once the validity of such observations is realized and accepted, significant changes will take place among the people who make up the church. Clergy and laity, ministers and church leaders, and hosts of Christians who differ from each other on such matters as race, sex, socioeconomic standing, and theological convictions may achieve a surprising coalescent harmony. After all, the true church is of God, by God, and for God.

# CREATION

There are few subjects over which the religious world is more divided than that of the creation. For many sincere people, the biblical story of the creation must be taken in its literal sense. If this is the correct point of view, it is understood that God operated on a twenty-four-hour day schedule for six successive days to complete the ultimate construction job of all time and eternity. If the whole narrative is to remain in a literal cast, then we may place the date for the creation as being slightly more than four thousand years ago. We must retain in mind the fact that a twenty-four-hour day requires an earth that has form and turns on its axis, a sun that shines, and a human being in a fixed position to chronicle the day. However, we note further that it was the second day before the earth had specific form, the fourth day before there was a sun in the sky, and the sixth day before the necessary human being was present to observe.

In sharp contrast, science tells the story of creation in other words. Science insists that the planetary system of which our earth is a minute entity developed from a shapeless mass of gas surrounding the sun. Further, our little earth is but a speck in an ever-expanding universe composed of millions of stars separated by a spatial expanse measured in light years. And what about the human race? Well, science says that we human beings have been around for at least one hundred thousand years. Is it difficult to understand why Christians often perceive science as a threat to biblical faith? It is appropriate to ask the question, "How do we reconcile this evident contradiction?"

Actually, we are in debt to the discoveries, experiments, and calculated observations of science. They have required us to distinguish between the vehicle of biblical revelation and its essential message. Slowly we have come to affirm that the Bible is not a scientific textbook.

It was never intended to be such. Our analytical questions pertaining to the origin of the universe and the origin of species can be answered by scientific investigation. What then, we may ask, do we learn from the biblical narrative? First, let it be clearly understood: *the Bible is a religious book—a theological book!* Therefore, the creation accounts serve to teach at least three ultimately important truths:

- God is the creator of the universe, the earth, all plant and animal life, and human beings.

- By divine intent, the created earth and life within and upon it are good.

- Further, we are intended to enjoy abundant life that is lived without fear.

Perhaps we commonly affirm the theologically valid essence of the doctrine of creation when we recite the ancient affirmation of faith: "I believe in God, the Father Almighty, Creator of heaven and earth." That is what the biblical narratives of creation teach. And that is what I believe! In other words, the Bible proclaims the *what* of creation. Science is concerned with the *how* and *when* of creation. There is no reason for us to confuse the two, but there is great need for us to understand and appreciate both of them.

# DEATH
## AND THE FUTURE
### OF HUMANKIND

There is a word that we are quite reluctant to use, especially when we are thinking of ourselves. That dreaded word is *death*. The scene is quite familiar. As our loved ones breathe their last, we make those difficult final *arrangements* to lay them tenderly beneath the sod. They are, in fact, taken from us. Although we may have shared with them in those common tasks and joys of life, we no longer hear their beloved voices and enjoy sweet fellowship with them. Death has invaded our domain, and we shall never be the same again.

There are some people who insist that the grave has the final word. They are able to offer certain substantiating reasons for their conclusion. After all, they may insist, none of us has witnessed anyone coming out of the grave. We all have seen bodies buried, but we have never seen one come forth alive from the grave. Frankly, personal experience seems to validate the notion that death marks the end for each of us.

The Christian faith does not deny such thinking *as far as the human body is concerned*. As a matter of fact, we agree *as far as the human body is concerned*. There is abundant evidence throughout the centuries of a universal belief in immortality. There must be something to it, for so many persons in so many places, cultures, and ages have affirmed faith in the idea. If only there existed some shred of historical proof?

We Christians believe that we have such proof. Jesus of Nazareth was crucified on a cross, and there he died. He was then buried in a tomb. On the third day, that tomb was discovered strangely empty.

Shortly thereafter, Jesus himself began to appear to his close friends. Later, he appeared to many others as well. Over the course of forty days, he appeared to many people. Then he ascended into heaven: It is quite remarkable how strong the proof is for the resurrection of Jesus, even for individuals who tend to question the divine inspiration of the scripture. In fact, there exists abundant early evidence for this event. For example, one carefully verified list of authentic witnesses is to be found in 1 Corinthians 15.

So, what does such reflection as this mean for the contemporary generation? Well, to state it theologically, our Christian faith in the future of redeemed humanity provides us with a limitless arena of an ever-growing measure of personality and spiritual freedom. In other words, Christians are energized by what Pierre Teilhard de Chardin calls *a great hope held in common.*

In summary, we admit that the thing we call *death* does bring to culmination our physical bodies in their present form. Nevertheless, the essentially important part of us, our souls—that is our unique personalities—continue to live on and on. So, what is death? It is merely a door into the full and abundant life of which Jesus spoke. It is not the end! *There is tomorrow!*

# DISCIPLESHIP

The evolution of learning is a remarkable experience. Take, for example, the process of our understanding the meaning of that familiar word *discipleship*. As children, we were introduced to that small group of people who forever *hung around with Jesus.* In those formative years of our lives, those men were identified as the *disciples* of Jesus. Somehow, I got the notion that they were little more than *errand boys for the boss.* Perhaps one of the lingering notions bestowed on me in those days was that there were twelve of them—and no more! After all, we were always hearing of the *twelve disciples.*

Eventually, we began to realize that the term *disciple* was not intended to be limited to twelve people who have been dead for two thousand years. In fact, it was quite surprising to discover that of the more than 230 instances of the term in the gospels alone, more than 90 percent are not limited to the twelve disciples! For example, consider the words of Luke 6:17 NRSV:

> And he came down with them and stood on a level place, *with a great crowd of his disciples* and a great multitude of people.

Well, there are many other passages just as suggestive of a much larger company of disciples. It might be concluded, therefore, that the words *disciple* and *Christian* are equivalent in nature and intent. So, it becomes appropriate to ponder what Jesus had in mind in establishing what we may call *the Order of Discipleship.*

The strategy of Jesus in calling individuals to follow him was to create a society of learners who would be willing to live with him, identify with his redemptive mission among people, change and mature in his fellowship, and obey his principles and guidelines of kingdom citizenship. From this understanding, the profile of discipleship becomes evident: The *disciple of Jesus* is that person who retains a passion for redemptive service, a willingness to participate in the cooperative enterprise of the kingdom of God, and a loving capacity for sharing the Christian life with other people.

Authentic discipleship was designed by our Lord. Like him, it is a timeless institution that is as relevant today as ever before. Indeed, discipleship is essential if the church is to prevail and succeed. By the way, that initial perception of the disciples of Jesus was accurate! More than ever, I am convinced that a true disciple is an *errand boy or girl for the boss.*

# ETERNAL LIFE

Here is a subject that has intrigued sage and seer, philosopher and theologian, the astute intellectual, and the average, run-of-the-mill individual. We all ponder the possibility of life after death even if we express our thoughts in contrasting language. I suppose that it is the inevitability of the end toward which we all move that prompts such reflection. In his accustomed provocative manner, Shakespeare challenges our thinking with these lines from his sonnet, "Time":

> Like as the waves make towards the pebbled shore, So do our minutes hasten to their end.

One will discover what may be called *Intimations of Immortality* throughout the scriptures. For most of us, there is the urge to seek the observations of Jesus regarding this and all matters of importance. So, what does he say about eternal life? For one thing, he promises eternal life to those who believe in him:

> For God so loved the world that he gave his only Son, that whoever believes in him should not perish but have eternal life. (John 3:16 NRSV)

Let us take the promises of Jesus at face value. We shall experience eternal life! What is the experiencing of eternal life? Dare we attempt an answer?

The moment has arrived when I must confess that I understand very little of this profound subject. I know what I believe about it. While I cannot prove what I believe, I believe it with all my being. Therefore, I shall attempt to share it with you. I believe that eternal life transcends this present existence. I am convinced that eternal life is time-inclusive, not time-concluding. Therefore, I believe that eternal life encompasses the future, the present, and the past. I believe that there are justifying moments to validate this view, moments when thoughts about the future are embraced with a certain sense of remembrance. You may refer to this as a simple instance of *a priori* actualization if you wish. But for me, it indeed is a profound return to the future! But above all else, eternal life is the awareness of personal oneness with the One who forever remains the Alpha and Omega, the sovereign First Cause, the Loving Redeemer incarnate in Jesus of Nazareth, the Lord God Omnipotent reigning forever, world without end!

I suppose that I would refer to the above statement as my personal credo pertaining to eternal life. Frankly, I have no difficulty at all in affirming my faith in the reality of immortality. In fact, it would be impossible for me to reject the idea of eternal life. Therefore, I close ranks with St. Paul and declare with conviction that "this mortal must put on immortality" (1 Corinthians 15:53 NRSV).

# FAITH

Mention of the word *faith* motivates long-standing religious concepts for all of us. After all, we have learned that *without faith, it is impossible to please God.* This familiar line introduces us to the role of faith in the religious experience. Yet the question remains as to what actually constitutes faith. Again, the author of Hebrews offers a definition: "Now faith is the assurance of things hoped for, the conviction of things not seen" (11:1 NRSV). This should be an adequate statement for the church. Sadly, that has not been the case!

Since the days of Martin Luther and John Calvin, classical Protestantism has insisted that our salvation is the result of our personal saving faith. In other words, faith is something that we must be found doing if we are to be saved from our sins. Actually, such thinking is not alien to the Old Testament legal requirements for gaining the forgiveness of God. Frankly, this perception borders on biblical heresy! The good news of the Christian religion does not declare that if we believe in God, he then will love us. Rather, the Christian message affirms that God loves us, so we need only have faith (trust) in his love.

Let us go one step further. Faith is unrelated to objective phenomenon. Faith is not required to affirm the existence of objects and events (i.e. miracles or signs). Such simply may be noted and accepted as factual. For example, I do not need to have faith in Jesus's healing of the blind man. I can see that he performed that ministry of compassion, and my faith in him is strengthened accordingly. St. Paul may have had this notion in mind when he observed that we "walk by faith, not by sight" (2 Corinthians 5:7 NRSV). In other words, faith is actualized in the life of the believer when the quest for the tangible evidence is surrendered.

In addition, it should be remembered that faith is not something that we initiate and develop. Rather, it is something that God initiates for us and in us. This is to say that faith is God's gift to us. If our faith emerged from the inner resources of our being, we would find ourselves in deep trouble in those seasons of personal doubt and skepticism. However, God gives us the faith to trust in his love for us, so our faith is not dependent upon our doubts, fears, skepticism, or ignorance. In many ways, even mature Christians are like immature children who constantly need to be assured of the love of parents. Therefore, God continues to intervene in loving demonstration of his saving love for us. That is why we have miracles and seasons of spiritual blessing as well as times of testing.

Through it all, the true believer is wise to reside in the Word of God. If we give our attention to the Word, remain obedient to its principles and precepts, and seek understanding thereby, we shall discover rather quickly that from the Word of God comes our faith in God. This enables us to renew our faith in God even though we reluctantly confess that there are times when we falter. The ultimate benefit of the believer's faith is that it cannot be lost! After all, God gives it to us again and again and again.

# FORGIVENESS

*Forgiveness* is a word that is immediately simple and complex at the same time. Our trouble with the word is that we know the definition, but we sense that there is more here than some academic explanation clarifies. In fact, *forgiveness* underscores the existence of some serious breach of attitude or conduct. The experience of forgiveness inevitably involves pain and the sacrifice of that precious commodity known as pride. If we are to begin to plumb the depths of the meaning of this word, we must examine it from the perspective of the forgiven and the forgiving.

If it becomes appropriate for me to forgive another person, it is understood that I perceive that person as one who has offended me. In so many words, I address that person (if only in my own mind) with some such declaration as this: "You have offended me in a serious way, and I would be justified in severing our relationship. You have wounded my pride and my principles. Nevertheless, you are an important part of my life, and I refuse to allow your action to abrogate our friendship. Therefore, I forgive you and ask you to remain my friend. I shall make an effort to forget the incident, and with God's help, we shall continue as before."

Such an approach may prove very painful to the forgiving party. But whoever said that forgiveness is an easy experience? Further, it should be noted that accepting forgiveness is also quite painful. After all, whether stated or not, to accept the forgiveness of another person is to admit that something very wrong has been said or done against that person.

Jesus has served us well in this regard when he gave us instruction regarding the matter of forgiveness in our prayers: "Forgive us our trespasses as we forgive those who trespass against us." I am impressed with the realization that, in Jesus's thinking, authentic forgiveness is without condition. A principle emerges here: Forgiveness that involves conditions is not forgiveness at all. Further, there is an attack on the issue of personal pride in the directive of Jesus. If our pride does not allow us to give unconditional forgiveness to others, that same pride will not allow us to receive forgiveness ourselves. Thus we shall remain prisoners locked in the padded cell of our own rigid attitudinal prohibitions.

Ultimately, forgiveness is the key that unlocks the door to personal and interpersonal freedom. As long as I wear the chains of bitterness toward any other person for perceived injustices against me, I shall never walk through life unfettered. Indeed, I am captive to my pride. In addition, the offender to my pride and principles will never be free to interface with me as in earlier times.

*O God! Please help us to give and receive forgiveness, remembering always the manner in which you freely forgive us in Jesus Christ. Amen.*

# GOD

"My friend, let me ask you a question. Do you know God?" This is the manner in which many zealous Christians initiate their efforts to evangelize or proselyte other persons to a particular brand of religion. Generally speaking, this is a very shallow and insipid approach to an exceedingly profound and transcendent subject. However, since the question has been cited, why not consider it? Indeed, is it possible to know God? I wonder.

Frequently, our music retains a larger measure of honesty regarding the subject of God than our pious homilies afford us. For example, consider the eloquent hymn familiar to most Christian congregations:

> Immortal, invisible, God only wise, in light inaccessible hid from our eyes, most blessed, most glorious, the Ancient of Days, almighty, victorious, thy great name we praise.

Do these lines suggest that knowing God is a simple process? I think not. Consider further the thirteenth-century ode to "The God of Many Names" by Mechthild of Germany:

> O burning Mountain, O chosen Sun,
> O perfect Moon, O fathomless Well,
> O unattainable Height, O Clearness beyond measure,
> O Wisdom without end, O Mercy without limit,
> O Strength without resistance, O Crown beyond all majesty:
> The humblest thing you created sings your praise.

So, the quest for God continues. Through the ages, "Getting to know you, getting to know more about you," has remained the theological diapason of the human species. After all these centuries, it seems that knowing God is dependent upon two cognitive streams of insight that we identify as *general* and *special revelation,* respectively. The knowledge of God derived from general revelation is the result of his self-disclosure in nature, history, and the evolving human itineration. In this regard, theological reflection flows from us toward God. We are seeking God.

In contrast, *special revelation* is a term indicating the ways in which God makes himself personally known to us. This process includes the salvation history that emerges from the story of Israel generally and Jesus Christ particularly. In addition, the Bible, God's sacred Word to humankind, teaches of the God who comes to us in the Law, the prophets, the wisdom writings, and Jesus of Nazareth. Further, the church of Jesus Christ remains the essential preserver and interpreter of that biblical record. In this instance, theological insight flows from God toward us. God is seeking us.

How about one more look at that provocative question that began this discussion: "Do you know God?" It is correct to respond, "I am getting to know him!" If we find ourselves pressed as to how we are getting to know God, we are free to declare, "I am getting to know God by means of natural knowledge and revealed knowledge."

# GOD THE FATHER

This is the age of the simple, straight-forward, *tell-it-like-it-is,* nontechnical language. We find ourselves pressured to relegate our religious imagery to the same objective precision, frequently forgetting that our religion is subjective. Therefore, much of the awe and grandeur of our religious faith becomes gradually diminished.

It is impossible to simplify a description or explanation of God. Nevertheless, we continue to try to accomplish this` *mission impossible.* Our best theologians prompt us to respect the subjective complexities of our religious imagery. After all, serious thoughts of God take place in the transcendent arena of subjective contemplation. Accordingly, it begins to penetrate our minds that the metaphor of the Fatherhood is integral to our Christian faith and heritage. Therefore, it never can be displaced by a casual or flippant attitude or approach. Still, we must remember that our use of the word *Father* is an anthropomorphic exercise in which we struggle to comprehend that which is beyond our understanding.

In a way, even the use of the word *Father* is to engage in a forbidden area. After all, the second commandment disallows our making God in the image of any earthly creature. Men and women are created in the image of God, but God is never to be made in the image of men or women. So, how dare we employ the earthly image of Father to describe the sovereign God of the universe?

A principle emerges here that will prove helpful: *All truth— especially truth which is given by revelation—must be perceived at the cognitive level if it is to be apprehended, assimilated, and applied in religious faith and social action.* Like Jesus before us, we reverently speak of God as our heavenly Father because we understand something of the love, security, and intimate fellowship implied in the term.

To quote Jesus, "God is spirit" (John 4:24 NRSV), and human images fall short of describing him. Indeed, the declaration of Jesus involves the perception of God as he essentially is: a universal, even a galactic deity, transcending time and space. We may be very grateful that Jesus also introduced us to God as our Father. Jesus found such language to be personally and spiritually helpful. I too find the image of Father to be helpful. Such reflections provide a continuing sense of security and of belonging.

*Our Father, who art in heaven, hallowed by thy Name.*

# GOD THE SON

On a certain day of profound significance for his disciples, Jesus made one of the most staggering statements ever recorded in literature: "Anyone who has seen me has seen the Father" (John 14:9 NRSV). This is a staggering observation when it is remembered that a very human man made the declaration. What did Jesus mean by the statement? Was he saying that he was God? What did his disciples understand his words to mean? It is interesting to note that those persons who knew Jesus best did not speak or write of his *deity* or his *divinity.* In contrast, they spoke and wrote about his actions. Their extant records indicate that they saw Jesus as a man who *acted* like God, doing those things that only God does. He was forever performing *miracles,* which the people believed were the prerogative of God alone. Further, he presumed the divine authority of forgiving sins. By word and deed, Jesus reflected the image of Redeemer, Savior, Judge, and Lord. Little wonder that the religious establishment of his day accused him of blasphemy because of his claiming that he was speaking and acting for God. Hence, the utter shock of his words: "Anyone who has seen me has seen the Father!"

Let us cut through further substantiating instances of Jesus's revolutionary words and deeds. It is appropriate for us to pose the question pertinent to our time and interest: *What was Jesus: human or God?* Surely, we can agree that there is a vast difference between humans and God. We understand that humans are finite, mortal, fallible, and limited to time and space. In contrast, God is perceived as infinite, eternal, omnipotent, omniscient, and omnipresent. So, which is Jesus? Is he on the human side or the divine side?

The only possible answer is that Jesus is both: human and divine! How is this possible? The church has not avoided this question. Through the centuries, it has been declared that Jesus of Nazareth was that very real human man in whom the essence of God was incarnate to such degree that he actually stood on the divine side. Thus, when we gaze beyond the limits of our own finitude and mortality, we see God in the face of Jesus. Accordingly, the words of Jesus make sense: "Anyone who has seen me has seen the Father!" Further, when Jesus looks upon the multitudes of his day, God is beholding humanity with all its needs. When Jesus speaks, God's own wisdom is revealed to us. Little wonder that his friend and disciple, St. Thomas, exclaimed, "My Lord and my God!" In other words, God has taken the initiative and bridged the gulf dividing humanity from divinity. He incarnated the person of Jesus, the carpenter from Nazareth, and enabled him to stand on both sides. Therefore, we can affirm our faith in Jesus as the anointed one, the messiah of God.

# GOD
## THE HOLY SPIRIT

A lengthy theological introduction to the Christian doctrine of the Holy Spirit will serve no good purpose. So, let us get right to the heart of the issue! Who is the Holy Spirit? Among the many biblical references to the Holy Spirit, perhaps we may discover a pertinent clue in one of the statements of Jesus:

> It is to your advantage that I go away, for if I do not
> go away, the Counselor will not come to you; but if I go, I
> will send him to you. And when he comes, he will convince
> the world concerning sin and righteousness, and judgment …
> When the Spirit of truth comes, he will guide you into all
> the truth.
> (John 16:7–8, 13 NRSV)

It seems to me that Jesus's promise is that the continuing and constant presence of God himself is assured. Surely this is a promise that should generate great joy among all Christians. Actually, many of us mainline Christians act as if we are afraid of the Holy Spirit. Perhaps, in this age of the objective and the tangible, we have surrendered our confidence in the supernatural, forgetting that the foundation of the supernatural is the Holy Spirit. Therefore, with certain exceptions, it is commonplace to affirm our collective and personal weakness in the doctrine and in the experience of the Holy Spirit.

How shall we become better acquainted with him? Actually, we learn of the Holy Spirit in the same way we learn of God the Father. We know him through his actions. Yahweh of Israel is the God who acts, and he has acted supremely and ultimately in the Christ event. In a related way, we learn of the Holy Spirit through his activity, which inevitably generates results, consequences, or, as Paul would say, fruit:

> But the fruit of the Spirit is love, joy, peace, patience, kindness, goodness, faithfulness, gentleness, self-control. (Galatians 5:22 NRSV)

It is essential that *this* particular doctrine be more for us than some vague, oblong blur. In other words, we must be clear and consistent as to the meaning of the Holy Spirit. If this essential doctrine of the faith is to have relevance for us, we must redefine its eternal significance. How shall we state it? Well, let us try the following:

> There are at least two virtually universal terms associated with the word *Spirit*. They are *intimacy* and *potency*. The Holy Spirit of God attests the immediately present action of sovereign deity. Accordingly, we come to understand that the Holy Spirit forever is God-near and God transcendent. Further, the Holy Spirit enables us to realize that our sovereign deity forever is God-at-hand and God-at-work.

So, what does this mean for us individually and as the people of God? The Christian who is devoid of a vital and vibrant possession by the Holy Spirit is a person who may be familiar with the forms of religion but lacks the spiritual energy essential to fulfill Christ's mission. Further, the church that is without the dynamic presence of the Holy Spirit is an entity congealed in the forms of antiquation and well on the way to spiritual impotence. In summary, the Holy Spirit is the divine reality of personal and collective Christian apprehension, and remains of ultimate importance for the urgent needs of each of us and all of us together.

# GRACE

Within the Protestant tradition, the word *grace* has retained a place of central significance. We may ponder whether we truly comprehend the nature and meaning of *grace* as it is presented in the New Testament.

May God grant that we all shall come to the place in our religious sensibility that we take this subject as seriously as did Bonhoeffer! So just what is grace? We can recall that favorite definition of our forebears: "Grace is the unmerited favor of God!" Well, surely it is that. However, it is far more than that! Our understanding of God's grace finds its Christian origins in the writings of Paul. As an example, consider the content of Paul's challenge to the Corinthians as he was seeking funds for the great collection that he intended to take to Jerusalem:

> For you know the grace of our Lord Jesus Christ,
> that though he was rich, yet for your sake he became poor, so that by his poverty you might become rich. (2 Corinthians 8:9 NRSV)

Emerging from this, and many other references as well, there are certain principles that explain the grand redemptive gift of God that we call *God's grace:*

1.  The self-revelation of God in the face of Jesus Christ is the clearest example of God's Grace. This is articulated by Paul in Romans 3:23–24 NRSV: "All have sinned and fall short of the glory of God, they are justified by his grace as a gift."

2.  The grace of God is further revealed in the way he reigns over the powers of sin and death through the death and resurrection of Christ. Again, Paul helps us here through his "Hymn on Adam and Christ," which presents Christ as the anti-Adam,

who comes to reign. Romans 5:15–21 is the passage. Just consider the conclusion: "Law came in, to increase the trespass; but where sin increased, grace abounded all the more, so that, as sin reigned in death, grace also might reign through righteousness to eternal life through Jesus Christ our Lord" (Romans 5:20–21 NRSV).

3.  The third component is the patience of God, which is pure grace. Peter explains this idea very well: "The Lord is not slack concerning his promise, as some men count slackness; but is long suffering toward you, not willing that any should perish but that all should come to repentance" (2 Peter 3:9 NRSV).

Is it possible to summarize a subject that is so transcendent? Well, perhaps not! Nevertheless, a simple and brief *apologia* is appropriate: *The grace of God is the objective intervention of God in the human process, by which he declares, "I have redeemed you; you are mine!"* Thus, it may be said that the redemptive act of Jesus on the cross is the redemptive act of him who was in Christ reconciling the world unto himself. That is the gospel of grace!

# GRATITUDE

We take it as our patriotic duty to become grateful, seriously grateful, at least once each year. In fact, we refer to this annual journey into the realm of collective gratitude as *Thanksgiving Day*. How altogether generous of us to remember to be grateful for the benefits of our lives at least one time each twelve months. I suspect that our reluctance to actualize in frequent and authentic expressions our sincere thanksgiving for God's benefits toward us is somewhat perplexing to the Almighty. If you doubt the Lord's desire that we cultivate grateful hearts, I suggest you give attention to the story of Jesus regarding the healing of the ten lepers (Luke 17:12–19). He questioned why only one of the ten took the time to return and say, "Thanks!"

When I was but a small child, I was introduced to the remarkable body of literature known as *Aesop's Fables.* One of my favorites is the story of Androcles:

> A slave named Androcles escaped from his master and fled to the forest. As he was wandering about there, he came upon a Lion lying down moaning and groaning. At first, he turned to flee, but finding that the Lion did not pursue him, he turned back and went up to him. As he came near, the Lion put out his paw, which was all swollen and bleeding, and Androcles found that a huge thorn had got into it, and was causing all the pain. He pulled out the thorn and bound up the paw of the Lion, who was soon able to rise and lick the hand of Androcles like a dog. Then the Lion took Androcles to his cave, and every day used to bring him meat from which to live. But shortly afterwards both Androcles and the Lion were captured, and the slave was sentenced to be thrown to the Lion, after the latter had been kept without

97

food for several days. The Emperor and all his Court came to see the spectacle, and Androcles was led out into the middle of the arena. Soon the Lion was let loose from his den, and rushed bounding and roaring towards his victim. But as soon as he came near to Androcles, he recognized his friend, and fawned upon him, and licked his hand like a friendly dog. The Emperor, surprised at this, summoned Androcles to him, who told him the whole story. Whereupon the slave was pardoned and freed, and the Lion was let loose to his native forest.

True to his custom, Aesop provides the ageless moral for his provocative fable: *gratitude is the sign of noble souls*. Surely, we can realize the value of this important emphasis. Both Jesus and Aesop point the way. The principle remains valid for all generations, especially our own: *gratitude is a way of life, not merely an event!* Now we have arrived at the central notion of the discussion: gratitude is the capacity to turn our attention from ourselves to the *source* of blessing to ourselves. Gratitude is the logical and perfect escape from the perpetual snare of introspective contemplation of personal virtues and progress. It is particularly true that when we are aware that we stand in the reality of the divine light, any possibility of shallow self-consciousness vanishes. Authentic gratitude is the capacity to negate the idea that personal blessings and benefits are self-acquired. Rather, it is the spirit of reverent affirmation of the mercy and grace of God.

Thus, it is appropriate that we attempt to unify the ageless moral with the applicable principle: *gratitude is the sign of noble souls*. Therefore, it is to be understood as a way of life and not merely an event.

# HEAVEN

Understanding the Christian religion depends, in large measure, on our understanding its symbols and images. For example, the sacraments of baptism and the Eucharist are made intelligible for us as we interpret the symbols of water, bread, and wine. However, certain components of our faith system elude the facility of tangible representation. Heaven, it seems to me, is one of those imponderable constituents.

As you may suspect, these observations are altogether personal opinion. So, think about them and then reach your own conclusions. Initially, many of my views on the subject of heaven are based on my personal logical frame of reference. For one thing, the prevailing notion of heaven as an everlasting church service has no appeal for me. After all, I have already experienced my share of those. Further, I have difficulty in thinking of heaven as some glorified monastery where we spend our eternity engaged in prolonged inner reflection. Above all, I cannot believe that heaven is a luxury retirement center for pious Christians living on a sanctified pension.

On a day of significance for his disciples, Jesus found himself speaking of the future in general and heaven in particular. We are quite familiar with one of his statements: "In my Father's house are many mansions." Indeed, we cherish that sentence, and it is a favorite of many of us. Another translation gives greater meaning to me: "In my Father's house are many stations." The idea of *stations* suggests development, evolution, progress. It lacks the sound of fixed immutability. This suggests, in turn, the limitless opportunity for creative life beyond life!

This is an incredible encouragement to all persons whose lives may have been terminated early, to those who may not have survived the birth experience, and to all people who may not have remained to hear their song sung, see their picture painted, or realize the actualization of their dreams. Just what is the point? Well, consider this: *In the eternal economy of God, the incomplete and inadequate manifestations of our destiny will be resurrected for perfection in that superlative sphere that we call heaven!* In other words, heaven is a spiritual state of creative and innovative activity, and we shall be quite busy doing the work of our Father. Such thinking as this prompts me to join the chorus of Robert Freeman:

> Shall I doubt my Father's mercy?
> Shall I think of death as doom,
> Or the stepping o'er the threshold
> To a bigger, brighter room?

# HELL

As youth gives way to the advancing years, so do the emotional and sensational emphases of evangelical dogma retreat before the forces of reason and revelation. It is particularly true that one tends to moderate traditional views of heaven and hell as one confronts the inevitable question we all ask, "What is going to happen to us?"

Let us consider the biblical lessons pertaining to hell. When carefully studied, we may be surprised to discover that traditional evangelical dogma runs counter to the teachings of Jesus. For example, it usually is held that heaven is the place where the *good people* go when they die, and hell is the place where the *bad people* go when they die. This sounds orthodox enough for sincere Bible-believing Christians like us! But is it the truth? What if the reverse is really the way it is?

Jesus remains the ultimate revolutionary in thought and action. Recall with me one of those occasions when he was speaking to the scribes and Pharisees (the recognized *good people* of that day) about hell. With provocative candor, the point is made: "Truly I tell you, the tax collectors and the prostitutes are going into the kingdom of God ahead of you" (Matthew 21:31 NRSV). That was not the only time that Jesus *ruffled the feathers* of creedal religion. He was forever pointing out that when the kingdom of God comes, there will be a dramatic reversal of position. The *outsiders* will become the *insiders,* and the *insiders* will be cast *outside.* Again, he insisted that in the kingdom of God, the *first* will become the *last.* It might be stated that in this manner of thinking, heaven is reserved for sinners, and hell will welcome the *good people.*

It becomes clear that we must interpret correctly the meaning of the respective images of heaven and hell. Accordingly, the notion of hell must be extrapolated from the mythology of Dante's *Inferno.*

Indeed, it is not to be understood in geographical terms at all. It is not a subterranean pit in the nether regions down under. Rather, it is to be understood as the continuing existence in dark isolation of the human personality as a result of the rejection of the redemptive power of love. Thus, it may be said that hell is the reality of eternal death, while heaven is the reality of eternal life.

Of course, the biblical record indicates that overt wickedness results in separation from God. For certain, that is hell enough for anyone! But we must not miss the central theological point of this discussion: *We must take seriously the salvation that God's grace provides us, for to attempt to measure up by our own merits is to fall short of the glory of God.*

In summary, I remain convinced that the creative intent of God will ultimately result in the salvation of all. I am unable to resist the compelling parable in which the good shepherd goes in search for the one lost sheep. Think of it! 99 percent is not enough! God wants all people to be safe and saved in his fold. So, the final word of the gospel is not damnation. It is salvation! And that is the gospel! Amen.

# JUDGMENT

As the years pass, increasingly I find myself in dialogue with many of the long-held theories that contribute to our creedal convictions. The notion of some *final judgment* that awaits each of us is but one of those theories so perplexing to me. This manner of thinking leads me to a rather provocative question: "Are all portions of the sacred scriptures of equal inspiration?" Personally, I have difficulty giving any portion of the Bible equal standing with the words of Jesus. For example, compare the respective observations of Paul and Jesus regarding the matter of *judgment:*

> We must all be made manifest before the judgment seat of Christ, that each one may receive the things done in the body, according to what he has done, whether it be good or bad. (2 Corinthians 5:10 NRSV)

> If any man hears my sayings and keep them not, I judge him not; for I came not to judge the world but to save the world ... the word that I spoke, the same shall judge him in the last day. (John 12:47–48 NRSV)

With all due respect for the beautiful and meaningful images and metaphors of the biblical record, I think that Jesus is indicating the transcendent reality of universal spiritual adjudication. Mortimer J. Adler has written a significant book entitled *Six Great Ideas.* He suggests that there are three ideas we judge by: *truth, goodness, and beauty.* Further, Adler contends that there are three ideas we act on: *liberty, equality, and justice.* If he is accurate, and I suspect that he is, then there is not one judgment day for us, but thousands! Every time we face the reality of truth, goodness, beauty, liberty, equality, and justice, our response to them is a judgment upon us. And I feel certain that God takes sovereign note of our response! Indeed, that is a double-edged judgment!

We find that it is difficult to close the subject at this point. What about the cumulative heritage of Christian dogma, which insists on some final or cosmic hour of divine review? Well, I don't know about such a concept. I certainly believe that Christ is the ultimate standard for all human conduct. How, therefore, will we be judged by him? Again, it may well be that we judge our own lives in the light of his perfect life. Such seems to be the intent of the lines by Whittier:

> We test our lives by Thine,
> Thou judgest us; Thy purity
> Doth all our lusts condemn.

Such thinking as we have engaged in today does not abrogate the eventuality of some *after- death judgment* encounter with God. Surely such an event will prove to be rewarding and altogether personally edifying. After all, it will be our privilege to stand in the presence of the One who is equipped to perfectly understand us, love us, and accord to us the beatific benefits of that home prepared for us by our Lord, Jesus Christ. Therefore, judgment is not an end toward which we progress with fear and anxiety. Indeed, it is the means by which we enter into God's eternal rest.

# THE KINGDOM OF GOD

In the ministry of Jesus, there is one phrase constantly employed. It is the phrase *kingdom of God*. In contrast, we rarely employ this phrase in our teaching and preaching. We may justifiably ponder the reason for this strange preclusion from contemporary theological discussion. Well, the very nature of what may be called *resurrection theology* defies modern thinking. After all, the phrase *kingdom of God* involves such words as *Lord, King, kingdom, triumph, rule, sovereign authority,* and *sovereign power*. Generally speaking, we are oriented to think in twits of democratic language. Therefore, the language of resurrection theology emerges as antiquated and irrelevant. Indeed, there are components of revisionist language that are intended to modernize and correctly interpret the authentic intent of God! We frequently hear the argument that archaic, hierarchical, and sexist language must be expunged.

Frankly, such words as *Lord, King, Ruler,* and similar terms are inherent to the biblical revelation. There are several principles involved here that merit our careful consideration. For one thing, the use of strong political language is no accident. Divine authority and power are the inescapable twins in the initiation and establishment of the kingdom of God. In other words, there are no other words or phrases adequate to explain the origin, nature, and extent of the kingdom.

Further, the kingdom of God has nothing to do with democracy. Jesus has not become Lord of lords and King of kings as a result of some political election. Jesus is Lord and King because God has so determined! Such was the conviction of the apostles:

> Therefore, God has highly exalted him and bestowed on him the name which is above every name, that at the name of Jesus every knee should bow, in heaven and on earth and under

the earth, and every tongue confess that Jesus Christ is Lord, to glory of God the Father. (Philippians 2:9–11 NRSV)

God has made him both Lord and Christ, this Jesus whom you crucified. (Acts 2:36 NRSV)

What terms would be appropriate to describe Jesus? How about *dictator? Chief executive officer? President?* Do these ideas fit? No! In no way do such words reflect the sovereign and divine nature of the King of the kingdom of God. To be candid, any language used to describe or define Jesus Christ and his kingdom remains altogether inadequate. It is appropriate, however, to continue such usage because it has achieved an acknowledged sacredness through centuries and generations of reverent and venerated service.

Therefore, we Christians gladly affirm our faith in the reality of the reign of our Lord, Jesus Christ. This is a reign that is simultaneously realized in the present expression of justice, love, freedom, and authentic humanity as actualized in the life and witness of the church, and in the essential transcendent reality of the future manifestation of Christ in his eternal glory.

# LIFE

Jesus once declared the purpose of his advent into the world with this statement: "I came that they may have life, and have it abundantly" (John 10:10 NRSV). I wonder what he had in mind when he spoke of life. Did Shakespeare capture the essence of Jesus's intent in his memorable reflections on life from Macbeth?

> To-morrow, and to-morrow, and to-morrow,
> Creeps in this petty pace from day to day,
> To the last syllable of recorded time;
> And all our yesterdays have lighted fools
> The way to dusty death. Out, out, brief candle!
> Life's but a walking shadow, a poor player
> That struts and frets his hour upon the stage,
> And then is heard no more; it is a tale
> Told by an idiot, full of sound and fury,
> Signifying nothing.
> (Macbeth 5.5.22-31)

It seems to me that Jesus had much more in mind with his *abundant life* than Shakespeare did in his imagery of life as a "walking shadow" or "poor, strutting, fretting player upon the stage." It is quite evident that the great playwright speaks of life as limited to the finitude of earthly struggle. In contrast, Jesus refers to the essence of qualitative eternal life. Such is the meaning of the grammatical formulations of the Greek text: "I came that they (people) may keep on having life eternal." Indeed, our Lord says as much in John 10:28 NRSV: "And I give them eternal life, and they shall never perish, and no one shall snatch them out of my hand."

Perhaps we have arrived at the basis for an authentic theological affirmation of the biblical meaning of the word *life*. In summary, it may be stated accordingly:

God is Life. Jesus is the very essence of that Life.

> Mankind is a minuscule fragment of that Life. Therefore, to be relevant, Christianity must be the actualization of that Life. As a matter of fact, Christianity will have no relation to God or humanity unless it is actualized Life in this age of spiritual darkness and dying. (*Christianity for Tomorrow*)

It is impossible to achieve the life of which Jesus speaks. It can only be received. It is a gift from God, and it is never earned—not even by our best efforts. Jesus declared, "I am the way, the truth, and the life." The message here is quite clear. Those who would experience life in abundance must experience Christ in faith. Any other approach results in death.

# LORD

Within the Christian community, there is little confusion regarding the use of the word *Lord*. As strange as it may seem to us, there does not exist such uniformity of opinion outside the Christian community. When we speak the word *Lord*, we generally refer to Jesus Christ. However, the majority of people throughout the world make no such concession. This should not be difficult for us to understand. After all, long before the time of Jesus, the people of Israel reserved the word *Lord* for their Creator God, the Lord God of Israel. It is appropriate, therefore, to raise certain questions regarding Jesus, God, and their relationship to each other.

Is there only one God, the *Creator of heaven and earth*? If so, is that one God the Lord and Savior of Israel? What about Jesus? If we affirm that in Jesus we may discover the Lord God of Israel present and at work, how can we avoid saying, in effect, that there are, in fact, two Gods? Is it possible that there are two Gods: one in heaven and one who visited in the flesh here on earth?

We might wish that the New Testament were a bit clearer on this point. In fact, the early church struggled with this matter for many years. Ultimately, in its effort to secure a solution to the problem, the doctrine of the *Trinity* evolved. Accordingly, Jesus came to be understood as *Immanuel: God with us* (Matthew 1:23 NRSV). In that last gospel to be written, the apostle John reflects the same conviction: Jesus, the *eternal Word*, has arrived to live among us in a flesh and blood human being. Ultimately, it is recorded that Jesus says of himself, "The Father and I are one" (John 10:30 NRSV). St. Paul reaches the same conclusion: "In him the whole fullness of deity dwells bodily" (Colossians 2:9 NRSV). Thus, it may be said that when we are introduced to Jesus, we are introduced to the Lord God. The church forever has proclaimed that

Jesus is infinitely more than a good man sent from God, more than a prophet, even more than an angel. Indeed, he is *God incarnate.* That is why the New Testament declares, in the words of the disciple Thomas, that Jesus is "My Lord and my God" (John 20:28 NRSV).

Since mention has been made of the evolving doctrine of the Trinity, a word about the Holy Spirit is in order. How does our notion of the Holy Spirit relate to the discussion of Jesus as Lord? Simply stated, when the flesh-and-blood Jesus no longer moves among us, his continuing presence abides. Thus, the transcendent, mystical, spiritual presence of the *Eternal God* is with his people as *the Lord Jesus* or as *Holy Spirit.*

In summary, the Christian doctrine of the *Lordship of Jesus* is really the doctrine of God himself. As such, we learn that within the Trinity there exists both *unity* and *distinction.* For example, while recognizing the reality of the words of Jesus that "the Father and I are one," we never forget that it is the Father who sends and the Son who is sent. Again, allow Jesus to explain: "The Son can do nothing on his own, but only what he sees the Father doing" (John 5:19 NRSV). The same distinction may be made regarding God the Creator and God the Holy Spirit.

Whoever said that Christian theology is simple?

# LOVE

There seems to be little question as to the best available definition of *love*. St. Paul provides it for us in his timeless presentation:

> Love is patient and kind; love is not jealous or boastful; it is not arrogant or rude. Love does not insist on its own way; it is not irritable or resentful; it does not rejoice at wrong, but rejoices in the right. Love bears all things, believes all things, hopes all things, endures all things. (1 Corinthians 13:4–7 NRSV)

We may thank God for the preservation of this clear statement on the meaning of love. Who among us is not aware of the plethora of confusions of *love* that dominate the popular culture of our time? Who is not sensitive to the emotional impulses, with their accompanying oedipal neuroses, which find their focus in the rock and pop lyrics of contemporary music expressions? Who doubts the existence of distorted and perverse attitudes pertaining to human relationships—all of which are justified by the prostitution of the word *love?* Again, we may thank God that we do have this clear statement of the meaning of authentic love.

As a matter of fact, the current confusion regarding *love* is so widespread that the simple statement of its meaning remains elusive. When one examines carefully the Corinthian text, there emerges a relational principle that allows a relevant definition for our day: *There are two facets inherent to authentic love: (1) the awareness of the worth and value of the other person, and (2) the resultant joy and happiness that that awareness provides.* In essence, Christian love enables one to delight unselfishly in the person and life of another while affirming his or her progress and success as much as one's own.

How do we do it? How do we love others as described by St. Paul? We must remember that such authentic love is born in the heart of God, not in us. Such love as we have discussed is not a *natural* human response. Rather, it is a *supernatural* expression. Accordingly, it can only exist when our hearts are conditioned by the presence and power of the Holy Spirit of God. Again, that is precisely the observation of the apostle Paul:

> Hope does not disappoint us, because God's love has been poured into our hearts through the Holy Spirit which has been given to us. (Romans 5:5 NRSV)

So how shall we summarize these thoughts? Well, think on these things: (1) Love is not a premeditated course of action. (2) Love is never the result of an accident: one never *falls in love,* as the saying goes. (3) Love is never the natural consequence of a cause-and-effect series of events. (4) Love is the spontaneous outpouring of the nature and presence of him of whom the scriptures attest that *God is love!*

# MINISTER

The popular image of the minister seems to have lost much of its luster in recent years. There are, I suppose, many possible reasons for the diminished respect rendered to the minister in our time. Part of the problem, as I see it, rests in the fact that society has made the minister into a *professional.* Since Jesus began this whole process of Christian ministry, it is fair to question whether or not Jesus would view the modem minister as a professional. In other words, if we want to understand the essential meaning of the minister and ministering, we must return to the norm for the minister and ministering. That norm is Jesus Christ the servant.

Messianic servanthood emerges in three distinct forms: *the apostle, the shepherd, and the priest.* In these forms, respectively, we discover the model for our corporate ministry as the servant-people of God and for the ordered ministry of those persons whom he sets apart as his servants of the Word.

*The apostle is the individual who is sent on a mission.* The apostle is an ambassador, a personal representative, an officer bearing a commission, an appointed delegate, a responsible courier, the messenger ordered into the midst of danger. In other words, the apostle is one who is sent. Again, our norm for understanding the apostolic nature of the minister is Jesus Christ. St. John states it quite clearly: "In this the love of God was made manifest among us, that God sent his only Son into the world" (1 John 4:9 NRSV). It is recorded that Jesus said as much about himself: "I came from the Father and have come into the world" (John 16:28 NRSV). Indeed, the authentic minister merits the respect and support of God's people. After all, the authentic minister is endowed with apostleship, and is sent among people to serve in Christ's stead. Further, the true minister is serving in response to a divine call: "And I heard the voice of the Lord saying, 'Whom shall I send, and who will go for us?' Then I said, 'Here I am! Send me'" (Isaiah 6:8 NRSV).

Again, the norm is Jesus Christ: "When he saw the crowds, he had compassion for them, because they were harassed and helpless, like sheep without a shepherd" (Matthew 9:36 NRSV). The responsibility for shepherding the Lord's flock literally defines the task of the minister. The service to which the minister is set apart includes the guardianship *(episkope)* of the Lord's flock, the care for the church, and the cure of the souls of her members. This is the service of the Shepherd, which is rendered in Christ's place. It is of significance that the word *pastor*, in its inclusive sense, designates the spirit of loving service for the flock of God. Still, under the guidance of faithful pastors, God prepares his servant-people for involvement in the world as the guardian community among all people. And all of this is accomplished in the spirit of the One who says, "I am the good shepherd. the good shepherd lays down his life for the sheep" (John 10:11 NRSV).

The authentic minister is an apostle and a shepherd. However, there is more. The true minister is priest as well. Remember that Jesus is our norm, and it is written of him that "We have a high priest ... Jesus, the Son of God ... Let us then with confidence draw near to the throne of grace" (Hebrews 4:14–16 NRSV). In his going out and coming in among the people served, the minister is a priest of Christ. This duty calls for the minster to represent God to the people and the people to God. This priestly ministry has no relationship to priestcraft as such, for the office served is temporary and culminates when the people served enter into the fullness of the new covenant. Subsequently, the minister will make the ultimate offering unto God, which is his faithful service in the world.

The authentic minister is due the respect of the people of God. After all, the authentic minister serves in the stead of Jesus Christ.

# MIRACLES

As a rule, our *enlightened* generation tends to reject or totally ignore the existence and validity of the supernatural or the miraculous. This should not surprise any of us, for the notions of history's critical thinkers during the past centuries have called into question all matters that did not conform to scientific measurement and logical evaluation. For example, Spinoza declares with conviction that miracles are impossible. Hume insists that they are incredible. Schleiermacher proclaims that the miracles are harmlessly relative. Although such instruction has caused many of us to hold such things as the miracles of Christ in suspicion, relegating them to the prejudiced enthusiasm of apostolic zeal, we must admit that the human race as a whole provides little evidence that we have evolved beyond faith in the reality of the miraculous.

The story of Jesus is replete with accounts of inexplicable miracles. The biblical record tells of such supernatural events as turning water into wine, the feeding of a vast multitude of people with a few fish and a few loaves of bread, walking on the water, calming the stormy sea, finding a coin in the mouth of a fish, etc. These, of course, are miracles having to do with nature. In addition, there were miracles of healing: *the man with the withered hand, cleansing of the leper, the healing of Peter's mother-in-law, the healing of the woman who touched the hem of his robe, the healing of the blind man, the healing of the paralytic, etc.* There were also miracles involving the healing of the mind (as seen in the case of the demoniac in the synagogue) and the raising of the dead (the daughter of Jairus, the widow's son at Nain, and, of course, Lazarus). In candor, these are stories that defy the reason of technologically and scientifically trained minds. What are we to do with them?

Frankly, I cannot accept as valid these intriguing stories unless I first accept the truth of the greatest of all miracles: the miracle of Christ himself! Once I have embraced in faith that God the Father Almighty, Creator of heaven and earth became incarnate in Jesus Christ, his only Son, our Lord, I have no problem whatever in affirming the historicity and validity of the miracles of Jesus.

Allow me to state differently the manner in which I am at peace with the miracle stories of the New Testament. *My faith is not the result of the stories of the miracles of Jesus. Rather, my confidence in the validity of the miracles results from my faith in Jesus Christ!* As a matter of fact, when reflecting on the divine nature of our Lord, we would be surprised if he had not accomplished something quite beyond the limits of pure reason. Therefore, I believe that Jesus restored sight to the blind, gave hearing to the deaf, made the lame to walk, and even raised the dead to life again. Ultimately, I believe in the resurrection of Jesus himself from the dead. Yes, I believe in miracles!

# PEACE

In biblical literature and present-day political and social dialogue alike, there is a word that retains significant prominence. That word is *peace.* In spite of all that has been written and spoken about it, I doubt that we have achieved an understanding of its ultimate meaning. The political pundits continue to extoll the importance of peace in world affairs. We are told that peace is in the interest of all nations and is at the bottom of the desire of all governments. Nevertheless, there continues the development of military armaments that are intended to guarantee the peace, but we realize that their constant increase is sapping the life and property of the nations. Instead of assuring peace, they are the prelude to a cataclysm in which the immense stored energy of destruction will finally be unloaded.

It was two thousand years ago that history's ultimate revolutionary made the following provocative observation: "Peace I leave with you. My peace I give to you; not as the world gives do I give to you" (John 14:27 NRSV). Indeed, there is something different about the kind of peace of which Jesus spoke. *My peace* is the bequest of Christ to his disciples as he prepares for his death and departure. In other words, he used a phrase that was actually the *shalom* of the Orient for greeting and parting. This is the term Jesus employed in his appearances after the resurrection (John 20:19, 21, 26). Without doubt, the *peace* of Jesus is spiritual peace, which only he can provide and which, in his incarnation, is made available to all people.

> Glory to God in the highest,
> and on earth peace among men with
> whom he is pleased. (Luke 2:14 NRSV)

It is exceedingly difficult to understand our own times. In the din of conflicting voices, both socially and politically, the eddying swirl of

117

ideological confusion inhibits honest and sincere efforts to actualize authentic accord among people. In no area of the human enterprise is there greater need for the divine intervention of Christ. So, in a word, what exactly is this *my peace* offered by our Lord?

*Eirene* means "peace with God and within humanity." It denotes order, the healing of all relationships. This *peace* is not a mutual relationship between God and humans that humans have designed. It is the relationship in which the believer is established in a faith attitude toward God. This relationship is the singular hope for the future of humankind.

> Now the God of peace be with you all. Amen. (Romans 15:33 NRSV)

# PRAYER

Prayer is a cumulative life of friendship with God
—Harry Emerson Fosdick

According to Jesus, by far the most important thing about prayer is to
keep at it.
—Frederick Buechner

He was praying in a certain place, and when he ceased, one of his
disciples said to him, "Lord, teach us to pray."
—Luke 11:1 (NRSV)

It seems to me that reflective religion is on the decline in our time. This is the *Age of the Activist,* and the benefits of speculative and reflective religion remain in short supply. We are impoverished to the degree that we prostitute the subjective integrity of the Christian faith before the shrine of social fad and fancy. Indeed, in many instances, the modes and methods of the church are determined by quasi-sociological polls that are formulated and designed to determine the direction of the populist winds of the day. Accordingly, even the worship of the sovereign God often reflects the influence of Broadway and Hollywood rather than the sacred traditions of the Judeo-Christian heritage. If such procedure is theologically and spiritually correct, then we may grieve for the misguided preachments of St. Paul. You do recall his counsel, do you not? Well, it goes as follows:

> Do not be conformed to this world, but be transformed by the renewing of your mind, that you may prove what is the will of God, what is good and acceptable and perfect. (Romans 12:2 NRSV)

The designated key for opening the door to the treasures of reflective and speculative religion is known as *prayer*. There is no need for a contemporary rock band to provide the proper mood for inner contemplation. Indeed, the sound and fury of such cacophonous distractions serve to thwart the essential freedom of intellect and spirit. The quest of the human spirit for existential friendship with God is diverted to an emotional response to environmental stimulus. Authentic prayer is made difficult, if not impossible, in that kind of circumstance. Did you notice that comment by Frederick Buechner? You know, I am speaking of the one that declares that "the most important thing about praying is to keep at it." Let's face it! It is frequently difficult to *keep at it* in this world of political, technological, and sociological distractions. So, what are we to do?

We must reeducate ourselves regarding the essential priorities of life. It is profitable to recall that we are not the first of Jesus's disciples who needed to learn to pray in an appropriate manner. It will not be offensive to the Almighty if we simply ask for divine help in this regard. The words of those earlier believers will do very well for us: "Lord, teach us to pray." I am certain that he will hear and answer such a request. Further, I am certain that the benefits of reflective and speculative religion will prove worth the effort.

# PREDESTINATION

It is good to examine briefly the word *predestination*. After all, most of us have heard the word used at one time or another. Likely, we did not understand the meaning of the word then, nor do we understand it now. Any person who has endured the rigors of theological education will recall those heated discussions in class over that provocative word. Again, we probably failed to achieve a definitive understanding then, and we probably have not achieved such an understanding now. So, one might ask, why bother with any further discussion on the subject? We bother because *predestination* is a biblical and theological word. Therefore, it must be significant. What do you think?

Many years ago, I asked an older minister to explain this term to me. He reminded me that the word *predestination* is frequently called *election*. He insisted that the two words mean the same thing. I have no reason to doubt his opinion. "Well," I pressed him, "tell me what election means."

Here is the classic response of that old preacher: "Election in the Bible is just like an election anywhere else. It simply means that the majority rules. In the Bible election, God has one vote and casts it for you. The devil has one vote and casts it against you. You have one vote, and however you vote determines the election!" Wow! That is simplifying theology for you!

To become a bit more precise, *predestination* (or *election* if you choose) is the view that God knows in advance whether we are going to heaven or hell. If it is true that God is all-wise, how in the world could one deny him such sovereign knowledge? However, his knowing what an individual is going to do does not inhibit, in any manner, that individual's freedom to do exactly what he or she chooses to do. Such thinking preserves the notion of *free will*.

121

Let us attempt one more approach, an approach that addresses the relationship between *predestination* and *human free will.* There exist two parallel theological bars in the biblical revelation. One is called predestination (or election), and the other is called human free will. The first declares, "No person comes unto me unless the Father draws him." The second proclaims, "Whosoever will may come and drink of the water of life freely." I think that I shall never understand fully the former, but the latter is quite clear to me. Therefore, I release the predestination bar and cling with all my heart to the human free will bar. In other words, I choose Jesus as my Savior because I am free to do so! After all, that is the way God planned it from the very beginning. See! He predestined my salvation! Oh me! This is too complex! But Amen anyway.

# RECONCILIATION

All of the words and phrases that we use in our Christian affirmations are not equal. The word *reconciliation* is of ultimate significance to us because it has to do with our salvation. Actually, it is such an important word that it is difficult to define in simple terms. Nevertheless, let us make an effort. It may be said that *reconciliation* refers to that peace we have with God, which is made possible by the sacrifice of Jesus Christ. This means that the disharmony and enmity that dominate the natural mentality of us all is removed, and an abiding spiritual concord prevails. It is clear that this is one of the cardinal doctrines of the Christian religion.

Perhaps it will be helpful if we attempt to simplify our definition of *reconciliation*. Think about it in this manner: *The message of reconciliation has God for its subject and humankind as the object to be redeemed.* Further, the ministry of reconciliation involves sharing in the sufferings of Christ and experiencing the reality of the Holy Spirit of God.

Since our *salvation* is explicit to the doctrine of *reconciliation,* let us look further. St. Paul is specific in his insistence that the message of the gospel is that we are called to be reconciled to God:

> So we are ambassadors for Christ, God making his appeal through us. We beseech you on behalf of Christ, be reconciled to God. (2 Corinthians 5:20 NRSV)

Such reconciliation has a profound consequence in our lives. As Paul indicates, "In him we ... become the righteousness of God" (2 Corinthians 4:21 NRSV). In his letter to the church in Rome, Paul underscores the notion that the nature of reconciliation as peace with God is actualized in the human response of faith, hope, and love

(5:1–5). Indeed, he summarizes with a profound statement: "God's love has been poured into our hearts through the Holy Spirit which has been given to us" (5:5 NRSV).

The present generation of enthusiasts for such matters as global ecology should be comforted in the realization that such always has been in the mind of God. The object of reconciliation is presented as being cosmic, personal, universal, and social. While the doctrine of reconciliation gives emphasis to the world, it focuses on humankind. However, it includes more than humankind. We note that in Colossians 1:19, reference is made to the object of reconciliation being "all things." In other words, the idea of "all things" refers to the universe: all that has been created by God.

How does one bring to closure such a profound doctrine? Well, perhaps the essence of simplicity is the order of the day. In direct terms, *the doctrine of reconciliation means that it is the purpose of God to fix the universe and everything that is in it.* Thank God! That includes us!

# REDEMPTION

Does it ever seem to you that we have a lot of religious words in our faith system that we frequently use without fully understanding their meaning? Such is the case for me. One of those large religious words is *redemption*. We have used it many times ourselves. Let us consider together its essential meaning.

After all has been said, in the final analysis, the word *redemption* simply means "freedom from death." As initially employed in the Old Testament, the word *redemption* refers the notion of national redemption. By the process of gradual theological evolution, it came to include the idea of personal redemption. This is clearly revealed in Job 19:25 NRSV:

> For I know that my redeemer lives,
> and at last he will stand upon the earth;
> and after my skin has been thus destroyed,
> then without my flesh I shall see God,
> whom I shall see on my side,
> and my eyes shall behold, and not another.

The doctrine of Redemption becomes fully developed in the writings of the New Testament. Jesus Christ is specifically portrayed as our redemption:

> He is the source of your life in Christ Jesus, whom God made our wisdom, our righteousness and sanctification and redemption.
> (1 Corinthians 1:30 NRSV)

Again, St. Paul presses this concept in his Galatian letter:

> Christ redeemed us from the curse of the law, having become a curse for us. (Galatians 3:13 NRSV)

> But when the time had fully come,
> God sent forth his Son,
> born of a woman,
> born under the law,
> so that we might receive adoption as sons. (Galatians 4:4f NRSV)

There is no doubt that it is the intention of God to secure the total redemption of humankind for the human experience:

> Redeem us from all iniquity and purify a people for his own who are zealous for good works. (Titus 2:14 NRSV)

The redemption of humanity is integral to the redemption of the whole created order:

> The creation itself will be set free from its bondage to decay and obtain the glorious liberty of the children of God. (Romans 8:21 NRSV)

We may conclude that redemption of the human body and the natural creation reflects the perfect unity between humanity and the creation itself, which has suffered from natural exploitation and human bondage to sin. It may be seen that humankind and creation are interrelated in depravation and in redemption as well. The ultimate good news of the gospel of redemption for us human beings is that, in the saving design of God, we are finally redeemed from the status of slavery to that of children of God:

> For you did not receive the spirit of slavery to fall back into fear, but you have received the spirit of sonship. (Romans 8:15 NRSV)

Little wonder that Christians love to proclaim in word and song, "Redeemed! How I love to proclaim it!"

# RELIGION

We should remember that *religion* and *Christianity* are not synonymous words. When used together, *religion* is the noun and *Christian* becomes the adjective. In other words, it is appropriate to refer to the *Christian religion.* Such a designation allows for the existence of religious systems that may be at variance with the Christian religion. The word *religion* is inclusive in that it may be applied to many and diverse faith expressions.

The word *religion* is a derivation of the Latin *religare,* which means "to bind fast." Generally speaking, *religion* refers to the set of beliefs and practices that characterize a given group of persons who cluster about an identifiable integrating center of conviction and commitment. Specifically, it should be emphasized that religion is response, not theory. We employ conceptual terms when speaking of religion for the essential purpose of description.

Since our primary focus is on the Christian religion, it will be good for us to summarize or describe its unique character. Actually, the Christian religion exists in the tension between creation and redemption. This, of course, corresponds to the religions of reason and the religions of revelation. To couch this notion in more familiar evangelical language, the Christian religion for many insists that to *have religion* is synonymous with having the *true religion*—that is the redemptive relationship with God through Jesus Christ. Accordingly, the Christian faith system evolves to encompass the following essential tenets:

- For our salvation, God became man in Jesus Christ. He died on the cross and rose again.

- No other alternative explanation weighs against the incredible story of the initiation and growth of the church.

- Ultimately, the story of the dying, rising God and the Christian Gospel is the declaration that the ascent of the human soul to God, by reflection and prayer, is met by the gracious condescension of God to our human estate.

Surely these thoughts describe the Christian religion. However, I wonder if it may not best be defined by its action? Well, consider the idea of James:

> Religion that is pure and undefiled before God and the Father is this: to visit orphans and widows in their affliction, and to keep oneself unstained from the world. (James 1:27 NRSV)

# REVELATION

In Christian theology, the word *revelation* refers to much more than that last mysterious book of the New Testament. Essentially, the doctrine of revelation has to do with the manner in which God makes himself known to us. Before we consider the broad relevance of the word, it will be helpful to determine its actual definition.

Accordingly, the word *revelation* is a Latin derivation that means "unveiling." In Christian theology, *revelation* translates the Greek *apokalypsis*. We recall that the final book of our Bible has the title *The Apokalypse (Unveiling) of Jesus Christ*. This same phrase is also employed to speak of the future visible return of Christ (1 Corinthians 1:7, 2 Thessalonians 1:7, and 1 Peter 1:7,13).

The biblical usage of the word *revelation* is not limited to the idea of the unveiling of an object or person. It also is used to the making known of a given truth. Again, in Christian theology, the doctrine of revelation is the doctrine of God's making himself, and pertinent truths about himself, available to humankind. In theological studies, the subject is divided into *general revelation* and *special revelation.*

General revelation involves the evidence for faith in God apart from Christ and the Bible. In this regard, reference is made to the role of human reason in religion. Accordingly, such intellectual disciplines as the philosophical arguments for the existence of God are involved (i.e. the ontological argument, the cosmological argument, the teleological argument, and the moral argument). There is an additional argument, *Consensus Gentium,* which has to do with the collective weight of all of the above.

*Special revelation* refers to three distinct ways God makes himself known to us: (1) in history, particularly the Christ-event; (2) in the sacred scriptures; and (3) through his people, the old Israel and the new Israel, which is the church of Jesus Christ.

# SACRAMENT

Many words are employed to explain, interpret, and amplify the Christian religion that do not originate in the scriptures. *Sacrament* is one such word. Before going further, let us recall the actual definition of the term. The word *sacrament* has its origin in the Latin word *sacramentum,* which, in turn, is a derivation of the Greek word *musterion (mystery).* Actually, in the New Testament, the Greek word *(musterion)* never appears in relation to any of the liturgical acts that we now identify as *sacraments.* Rather, it is used to reflect the ways in which our Lord makes known hidden dimensions of reality.

In the long progression of the Christian Church, seven rites have been called *sacraments.* They are Baptism, the Lord's Supper, Confirmation, Penance, Holy Orders, Marriage, and Extreme Unction. To the present day, the Roman Catholic Church recognizes all seven. However, Protestant churches hold that there are only *two* sacraments: Baptism and the Lord's Supper. This latter fact is the result of the Protestant conviction that certain requirements must prevail to authenticate a religious rite as being identified as a *sacrament:*

1. *A sacrament must be the result of divine designation.* In other words, worship in every aspect must be authenticated by the commands of God. Consider these specific directives:

   Go therefore and make disciples of all nations, baptizing them in the name of the Father and of the Son and of the Holy Spirit. (Matthew 28:519 NRSV)

   For I received from the Lord what I also delivered to you, that the Lord Jesus on the night when he was betrayed took bread, and when he had given thanks, he broke it and said,

"This is my body which is for you. Do this in remembrance of me." (1 Corinthians 11:23–24 NRSV)

2. *Authentic sacraments retain certain signs that are sensitive to sight and touch.* Words alone are inadequate. However, the spoken word should be employed to accompany the sensible signs.

3. *The sacraments communicate redemptive content because they are administered by divine appointment of God.* This is to say that while the sacraments do not provide our salvation, they are linked to it.

4. *The sacraments constitute a pledge to those persons receiving them.* It should be remembered that *circumcision* in the Old Testament (which parallels to *Baptism* in the New Testament) is identified as "a seal of the righteousness of faith" (Romans 4:11 NRSV).

5. *A sacrament is a ritual of participation.* The witnessing of a sacrament does not possess intrinsic redemptive value. In other words, the respective elements of the sacraments must be applied on the basis of their nature if they are to serve to seal the spiritual benefits that the sign indicates.

In summary, what does this mean for us? Simply stated, God is eternally aware of our finitude and needs. Therefore, as an act of grace, he has ordained the sacraments so that we may perceive, in tangible ways and means, his presence and promise.

# SALVATION

The word *salvation* is one of the dominant terms employed by Christians of all persuasions throughout the world. Perhaps it is so broadly employed that it is one of those taken-for-granted words that has lost some of its true significance. Yet we all would agree that it remains one of the essential components of our common faith. Therefore, it is important that we understand its true meaning.

The Greek word for *salvation (soteria)* is found about fifty times in the New Testament. Its meaning is quite varied, and it is used to denote deliverance, preservation, and salvation. In this sense, its application may be applied (a) to material and temporal deliverance from danger and apprehension; (b) to the spiritual and eternal deliverance provided by God to all who receive by faith his conditions of repentance of sin and faith in the Lord Jesus Christ, and confess him as Lord; (c) to the present experience of God's power to deliver from the power of temptation and sin; and (d) to the ultimate redemption of believers at the Second Coming of Christ for all his saints.

The doctrine of salvation is based upon a reasonable process. Salvation originates in God, "For there is one God." There exists one mediator between God and the human race, "the Man Christ Jesus" (1 Timothy 2:5 NRSV). Ultimately, "There is no salvation through any other name" (Acts 4:12 NRSV). The process itself underscores the principle that salvation is only and exclusively in Jesus Christ.

Let us not ignore a vital evangelical question: *How does one experience salvation?* There are about 115 passages that base salvation on believing alone, and there are about 35 which simply refer to faith in Jesus Christ. Sadly, we zealous Christians frequently add conditions of our own: believe and repent, believe and be baptized, believe and confess sin, believe and publicly confess Christ, believe and work to live a better life, believe and pray for salvation in the world to come.

In summary, the salvation provided by our Lord is inevitably eternal in duration. This is due to the fact that salvation is always and altogether a work of God. We believe that his purpose and power never fail: "And I am sure that he who began a good work in you will bring it to completion at the day of Jesus Christ" (Philippians 1:6 NRSV).

# SATAN

The tragic events of history during the last century have nudged our thinking in the direction of a theological dualism. Some explanation is needed for the unbridled tides of famine, war, poverty, disease, and social violence that have swept across the human landscape. Therefore, well-intentioned and thoughtful Christians have struggled in the tension between belief in a singular, good, and sagacious Being, and two equal, uncreated, antithetic powers: one ultimately good and the other ultimately bad. We hasten to identify ultimate good with God the Father Almighty, and we are quick to designate ultimate bad with a supernatural being known as *Satan*. What do we really know about Satan?

The biblical picture of Satan is best perceived as a mural of evolutionary process. The term is used in the Old Testament to describe the person and work of either a human or superhuman adversary, or one who obstructs or accuses in some form of a legal setting. Later Old Testament writers project Satan as the archenemy of God, an evil spirit who was opposed to God and who led demons and evil spirits in a way against God and his followers.

In the New Testament, the presence and power of evil in the world is attributed to the figure of Satan. Actually, the word *Satan* is a transliteration of the Hebrew word for adversary, enemy, or one who obstructs. Although the biblical references describing the role and functions of Satan are varied and many in the New Testament, the primary functions seem essentially to be two:

1.  Leadership of the forces of evil
    But when the Pharisees heard it, they said,
    "It is only by Beelzebul, the prince of demons,
    that this man casts out demons." (Matthew 12:24 NRSV)

And the Scribes who came down from Jerusalem said, "He is possessed by Beelzebul, and by the prince of demons he casts out the demons." (Mark 3:22 NRSV)

2.  Opposition to Christ and the church
    Put on the whole armor of God that you may be able to stand against the wiles of the devil. For we are not contending against flesh and blood, but against the principalities, against the powers, against the world rulers of this present darkness, against the spiritual hosts of wickedness in the heavenly places. (Ephesians 6:11–12 NRSV)

The summary observation of the New Testament regarding Satan is that Jesus will finally triumph over him. Indeed, that triumph is both a present reality and a future certainty. To state the matter differently, although the power of Satan is not completely abolished, it already is broken:

And I heard a loud voice in heaven, saying, "Now the salvation and the power and the kingdom of our God and the authority of his Christ have come, for the accuser of our brethren has been thrown down, who accuses them day and night before our God.
And they have conquered him by the blood of the Lamb and by the word of their testimony, for they loved not their lives even unto death." (Revelation 12:10–11 NRSV)

Now, back where we started! The notion of a philosophy of dualism may retain a certain intellectual appeal. However, it may be said with conviction that *there is no biblical evidence for such thinking!* Rather, the final word on this matter rests with the judicious imagery of a final disposition of the person and power of Satan:

And the devil who had deceived them was thrown into the lake of fire and sulphur where the beast and the false prophet were, and they will be tormented day and night for ever and ever. (Revelation 20:10 NRSV)

# THE SECOND ADVENT

Jesus is coming again! Before we go further, let us honestly admit that there are some people who call themselves Christians who do not agree with this statement. For some people, Jesus of Nazareth was merely a good man, a great man, a worthy example for all people, but only a man. He died as a martyr, and that was the end of Jesus. No resurrection! No return to earth again! This is a radical interpretation of the biblical revelation and is an open contradiction of the New Testament at many significant points. Thankfully, this view has never gained universal acceptance and remains alien to the position of historic Christianity.

The blessed hope of the Second Coming of our Lord is not the provincial monopoly of a small extreme fundamentalist segment of Christians, as some would have us believe. Rather, the vast majority of all Christians throughout all the ages believes that Jesus is coming again. Bible-believing Christians may hold different views about such things as the millennium—some pre-millenarians, some post-millenarians, and some non-millenarians—but most unite in their common conviction that Jesus is coming again.

The idea of a Second Coming of the Messiah does not appear initially in the New Testament. As a matter of record, the Old Testament predicted two distinct advents of the Messiah. On one hand, there were those glorious prophesies of the triumphant appearance of Israel's Messiah to establish on earth the true kingdom of God. On the other hand, there was a different prediction, often ignored by many people in ancient times, of a coming of the Messiah in humiliation and suffering.

Who can ignore the graphic picture of the face of suffering found in Isaiah 53:1–3 (NRSV)?

> Who has believed what we
> have heard?
> And to whom has the arm of the
> Lord been revealed? -
> For he grew up before him like a
> young plant,
> and like a root out of dry ground;
> he had no form or majesty that
> We should look at him,
> . . . and no beauty that we should desire him. He was despised
> and rejected by men;
> a man of sorrows and acquainted with grief, and as one
> from whom men hide their faces, he was despised and we
> esteemed him not.

The first coming of our Lord was in humiliation to make atonement for our sins. The other predictions of the Old Testament about his coming in glory remain to be fulfilled. To those Old Testament predictions are added many more precise ones in the New Testament. Let us consider a few of the many:

> For as the lightening comes out of the east, and shines even
> unto the west; so shall also
> be the coming of the Son of man. (Matthew 24:27 NRSV)

> And they shall see the Son of man coming in the clouds of
> heaven with power and great glory. (Matthew 24:30 NRSV)
> And if I go and prepare a place for you, I will come again,
> and receive you unto myself; that where I am, there you may
> be also. (John 14:3 NRSV)

> You men of Galilee, why do you stand gazing up into haven?
> This same Jesus, who is taken up from you into heaven, shall
> come in like manner as you have witnessed him go into
> heaven. (Acts 1:11 NRSV)

> For the Lord himself shall descend from heaven with a
> shout, with the voice of the archangel, and with the trumpet
> of God. (1 Thessalonians 4:16 NRSV)

So Christ was once offered to bear the sins of many; and.
unto those who look for him shall he appear
the second time without sin unto salvation. (Hebrews
9:28 NRSV)

Behold, he comes with clouds; and every eye shall see Him.
(Revelation 1:7 NRSV)

As previously indicated, these are but a few of the many passages concerning the Second Coming of Jesus that appear throughout the scriptures. There need be no doubt in the mind of any Bible-believing Christian that Jesus is coming again. Of course, there remain a few minor points regarding the Second Coming about which we fail to see eye-to-eye. However, we are able to unify around the certain conviction that we agree on the things of authentic importance. Accordingly, we remain committed to the principle that minor differences must not obscure for any of us the blessed hope of the Second Coming of our Lord, or disrupt our fellowship as Christians.

# SERVICE

A provocative question found its way into my reflections the other day: If Jesus of Nazareth were to make a personal visit to the churches of America, would he recognize the religious formulations of our congregations and denominations as having any significant relationship to the church he founded? Well, what do you think?

Practically speaking, religion in general is frequently absorbed in processes that are virtually unrelated to the issues of the real world. So, we give stirring emphasis to stewardship (the essential requirement to sustain our institutional monuments). We persist in saying our self-centered prayers. We celebrate our pilgrimages to Jerusalem, Mecca, or Rome. We kiss our sacred stones, count our prayer beads, say our rosaries, crawl up our sacred steps, and take countless other measures that fall short of accomplishing the humble mission exemplified by our Lord, who said, "I am among you as one who serves."

Sir Winston Churchill is reported to have made a startling statement: "We structure our institutions, and forever afterward our institutions structure us!" Perhaps that is what the old Hebrew prophet had in mind:

> Wherewith shall I come before Jehovah, and bow myself before the high God? Shall I come before him with burnt-offerings, and calves a year old? Will Jehovah be pleased with thousands of rams, or with ten thousands of rivers of oil? Shall I give my first-born for my transgressions, the fruit of my body for the sin of my soul? He hath showed thee, O man, what is good; and what doth Jehovah require of thee, but to do justly, and to love kindness, and to walk humbly with thy God. (Micah 6:6–8 ASV)

As long as the only religion we know anything about is practiced within the sanctified security of stained-glass elegance wherein we mouth ancient creeds and sing with blended zeal the affirmations of our faith perceptions, while squalor, ignorance, and shameful indulgences abound unabated outside, we may be certain that we have little in common with the servant Messiah, Christ. We will profit greatly if we recall that when God the Father Almighty set his hand to write his redemptive creed for *all* people, he did it in the serving, suffering, and dying blood of Jesus, the Son. Perhaps the time has come for us to try once more. Maybe this time we shall observe God's directive as written by his servant, Amos:

> Take thou away from me the noise of thy songs; for I will not hear the melody of thy viols. But let justice roll down as waters, and righteousness as a mighty stream. (Amos 5:23–24 ASV)

Jesus had a brother. As he neared the end of his life, James thought often of the service ministry of his brother and Savior. Accordingly, one of his memorable observations is retained for our benefit. For the sake of our souls, let us consider it again:

> What good is it, my brothers and sisters, if you say you have faith but do not have works? Can faith save you? If a brother or sister is naked and lacks daily food, and one of you says to them, "Go in peace; keep warm and eat your fill," and yet you do not supply their bodily needs, what is the good of that? So faith by itself, if it has no works, is dead. (James 1:14–17 NRSV)

To say the least, authentic religion—the religion of the Bible—insists that service to other people who are in need of our care is the essential actualization of redeeming faith. We may conclude, therefore, that the Christian religion is best symbolized by the cross and the towel.

# SIN

How shall we discuss the subject of *sin* in an age when the word has fallen into such general social disrepute? In other words, contemporary views of sin have little in common with the religious views of sin prevalent in earlier generations. Therefore, why not attempt a different approach?

Are we able to recognize that something is wrong in our cities, nations, and the world in general? To what extent is environmental pollution a symptom of our social sin? What is the meaning of the skies that have become darkened over our population centers? What is the essential cause of the disease-laden pollutants and sediments that render our lakes and rivers unsafe for fishing or swimming? What do you choose to call it when the vast majority of earth's consumable products are used and hoarded by a miniscule fraction of earth's population? Dare we mention such indulgences as extra and premarital sex, the profusion of parental irresponsibility, pervasive child abuse, the epidemic of moral perversion, and the insidious malaise of crass pornography? What are we to call such turpitude of the Judeo-Christian religion?

There is a word for what we have described. Admittedly, it is a biblical word. It is a word employed by Moses, the prophets, Jesus, the apostles, and serious devotees of the Word and will of God down through the centuries. That word is *sin.* If we truly are the people of the Book, why do we avoid use of the word? In 1863, Abraham Lincoln, America's greatest and most theological president, issued a call for a National Day of Prayer, and in it he used the word *sin:*

> It is the duty of nations as well as of men to own their dependence upon the overruling power of God, to confess their sins and transgressions in humble sorrow, yet with

assured hope that genuine repentance will lead to mercy and pardon.

Let us refresh our memory! What has been the historic perception of the church regarding sin? To put it succinctly, it may be stated as follows: *sin is the self- destructive abrogation of a right relationship with God and other people.* Such abrogation may occur as a result of: (1) disobedience to the law of God; (2) surrender to the magnetism of fleshly sensuality involving the natural physical needs, desires, and pleasures; and (3) the egotistical drive to be good (to be like God), which is the essential root of sin.

Yes, something is wrong in our cities, nations, and the world in general. Symptoms of the problem are legion. We shall never "fix" the symptoms until the problem itself is fixed. The problem is *sin.* The problem can be fixed by following a very clear directive:

> If we confess our sins, he is faithful and just, and will forgive our sins and cleanse us from all unrighteousness. (1 John 1:9 NRSV)

# SUFFERING

"Is anyone among you suffering?" (James 5:13 NRSV). We might imagine that virtually everyone would respond in the affirmative to this question. Certainly, it is true that each of us, during the process of living, will experience suffering of one kind or another. The fact that suffering is a universal phenomenon does not soften its harsh impact on us when it is our lot to be victimized by its negative presence. More often than not, we will fail to comprehend why we should be subject to such a painful process. "What have I done to deserve this?" is a commonly voiced question. Indeed, "Why me?" Is there an adequate answer to the provocative query, "Why do the righteous suffer?"

Since likely it is true that any answer offered will prove to be insufficient, let us attempt a different approach. Let us consider the notion that human suffering is best understood by not focusing on some human error in act or judgment, but it is best seen in the light of God's ultimate purpose for us. While this line of thinking may seem of little comfort at first glance, it may provide us with a firm, rational basis in our endless struggle to make sense out of misery. In other words, a meaningful explanation begins with God.

Reflect on the idea that God, who created us, knows who we are and what we are. Further, he is quite sensitive to the fact that our ultimate happiness is to be found in him. It may be that in the process of actualizing abundant or moderate success, prosperity, and personal pleasure, we fail to surrender to God what we may perceive to be *our own lives*. In other words, in the process of counting our many blessings, we are failing to blessing of *being found in him*. Such an approach may speak to the kinds of suffering familiar to the relatively prosperous citizens of the United States. However, it does not touch everyone everywhere.

What about the disease-ridden third-world countries? What about the very young, the very old, the very helpless? If we attempt to measure all suffering by the explanation just suggested, God is turned into some kind of intemperate purveyor of misery and pain. We must be willing to admit that there does not exist adequate explanations for all forms of human suffering. Indeed, it seems that some of it is altogether meaningless. This inevitable blight on the human experience wears many and varied garments. It comes to some in the dress of totalitarian cruelty. Others discover that they have adorned themselves with the binding chains of self-inflicted stupidity. It would be additional stupidity to blame God for such travesties of human folly. Perhaps, it is time for us to determine if some positive conclusion may be drawn from such a negative factor. In other words, is there anything available to God or us that may be redemptive in the reality of suffering?

Consider the notion that the ultimately important question regarding suffering is not, "Why do the righteous suffer?" It may help our thinking if we pose another question: "What is to be learned from the pain and the travail of the situation?" Indeed, when we determine to take from the experience principles and lessons for living, serving, and dying, we succeed in neutralizing the dehumanizing influence of suffering and affirm the character, integrity, and purpose of living. In so doing, the emptiness and defeat of suffering are transformed into meaning and purpose, and the end result is the blessed discovery of the presence, power, and peace of God.

# TEMPTATION

Generally speaking, when the word *temptation* is used, images of the Garden, the primeval man and woman, and a wily snake come to mind. Indeed, we are so familiar with this story that it has become for us little more than a sanctified fairy-tale. Nevertheless, it remains an early description of the reality of negative influence. As such, we are reminded that we are prone to be tested or tried in ways that challenge the intent and integrity of God. In the Genesis account, negative temptation appears in the form of insinuating questions designed to arouse doubt as to the goodness of God: "Did God really say, 'You shall not eat of any tree of the garden?'" For God knows that when you eat of it your eyes will be opened, and you will be like God." The nature of negative temptation remains constant. To this very day, we struggle to resist the appeal to the physical and material (good for food), the appeal to vanity (pleasant to the eyes), and the appeal for greater knowledge and power through the experience of evil.

The New Testament word for *temptation* possesses a positive aspect as well as negative. For example, it is often used in reference to trials with a beneficial purpose and effect:

> You are those who have continued with me in my trials; and I assign to you, as my Father assigned to me, a Kingdom, that you may eat and drink at my table in my Kingdom, and sit on thrones judging the twelve tribes of Israel. (Luke 22:28–30 NRSV)

> Blessed is the man who endures trial, for when he has stood the test he will receive the crown of life which God has promised to those who love him. (James 1:12 NRSV)

It is good for us to reflect on other very practical applications of positive temptation. It is physically beneficial to yield to the temptation to eat properly and exercise regularly. It is mentally beneficial to yield to the temptation to read the great literature of the ages. It is psychologically beneficial to yield to the temptation for thought and life that contribute to personality wholeness. It is aesthetically beneficial to yield to the temptation to develop a sensitive appreciation for great music, great art, and great architecture. It is spiritually beneficial to yield to the gentle persuasion to respond to the call of God in personal life.

Clearly, there is temptation in every life. The question for each of us is whether we shall yield to the dubious inducements of the vipers of negation or respond redemptively to the bright seraphs of faith, hope, and love.

# TROUBLE

The universal malaise which befalls all of us is called *trouble*. As a result, certain questions are universally found among all people: "Why? Why must this happen to me? Why must I suffer so? What have I done that I should endure this trouble?" Rabbi Harold Kushner addressed many of these questions in his provocative book, *When Bad Things Happen To Good People*. So it is that we all struggle with such troubles as illness, injury, rejection, financial failure, marital disappointment, and ultimately death. The moment has arrived to pose the question introduced by Job and repeated by millions throughout history: "Why do the righteous suffer?"

A definitive answer to the question of trouble eludes us. Trouble exists. We all experience it. Therefore, is there a Christian response adequate for such severe tests in life? Certainly! The faith of the Christian exclaims with confidence that God has a word for us: "I will be with you always!" Such was the conviction of St. Paul. Consider again his affirmation of assurance found in his letter to the Romans (8:35 NRSV):

> Who shall separate us from the love of Christ? Shall tribulation, or distress, or persecution, or famine, or nakedness, or peril, or sword?

Well, that covers many, if not most, of the troubles that we face in life. I doubt if there exists a person who does not have something in his or her individual experience that personal preference would eliminate. Indeed, trouble abounds in our lives: exhausting, frustrating, exacerbating, debilitating, and disquieting trouble! Simply stated, if you are not experiencing trouble today, be patient! You will be in the near future.

Does God have a word for us regarding our days of trouble? As a matter of fact, he does! Allow the apostle Paul to tell us about it:

> In all these things we are more than conquerors through him who loved us. For I am sure that neither death, nor life, nor angels, nor principalities, nor things present, nor things to come, nor powers, nor height, nor depth, nor anything else in all creation, will be able to separate us from the love of God in Christ Jesus our Lord. (Romans 8:37–39 NRSV)

There you have it—the conclusion of the matter! The troubles of life, tragic or tedious, are powerless to invalidate the love of God in Christ Jesus, our Lord. By the way, as a final and practical word of encouragement, I remember the sage counsel of the great Canadian theologian, Manford George Gutzke: "When you think that you are in the middle of trouble, it is good to know that to be in the middle is to be halfway through it!" (Delivered in a classroom lecture at Columbia Theological Seminary, 1956).

Amen!

# TRUTH

I am the truth.
—Jesus
(John 14:6 NRSV)

Many years ago, when I first dipped my feet in the water of classical philosophy, I was introduced to the idea of the intellectual quest for truth. We spent many exciting hours discussing the competing philosophical theories pertaining to the ascertaining of truth. Well do I recall the intellectual energy expended in our exploring those two best-known theories of truth: the correspondence theory and the coherence theory. In simple terms, we entered into the debate as to whether truth is derived from sense experience or the exercise of pure reason. As you might suspect, we came no closer to fixed conclusions than did our intellectual mentors: Kant, Descartes, Locke, Hume, and the like.

The quest for truth is no recent academic process. Recall that Pilate posed for Jesus that provocative question: "What is truth?" (John 18:38 NRSV). Why is it so very difficult for us to realize that the age-old search for absolute truth is really not such an elusive phantom? Why do we hesitate to hear, examine, test, and evaluate the direct statement of the Galilean? Observe his statement as if for the first time: "I am the truth." Now, what are we to make of this declaration?

In the first place, we do well to attempt a theological definition (as compared to a philosophical definition). Accordingly, it may be stated that *truth is a quality of judgment reached as a result of the total witness of facts and individual and collective experience.* Perhaps this idea may be stated in a very elementary form: *Truth inevitably corresponds to things as they actually are, logically and experientially.*

As Christians, we affirm that Jesus Christ is the essential extension of God the Father Almighty. Therefore, we further affirm that Jesus is truth because he forever is the author of fact and meaning. It becomes possible at this point for theology to converge with philosophy and summarize that *authentic truth is truth because it corresponds with the mind of God.*

To truly be redemptive, theology and philosophy must be fleshed out in existential human experience. Now the comments become quite personal. I remain personally committed to the Christian faith and Jesus Christ for two reasons altogether meaningful to me: (1) The history, teachings, works, sacrifice, and resurrection of Jesus are the *validated expressions* of God's divine purpose in the human saga, and (2) I have personally experienced the indwelling presence of the living Christ for more than a half-hundred years. That is good enough for me. Jesus said, "I am the truth." Thank God, I know it to be the truth!

# UBIQUITOUS

*Ubiquitous!* This is one of the ultimately important words for the person who desires to understand the ultimately important topics of *God* and *prayer*. As few other words available to us, *ubiquitous* defines one of the essential attributes of God while clarifying for us the nature and possibility of authentic prayer. So, let us consider how the word defines God. Actually, *ubiquitous* is a many-faceted word. It is an adjective that modifies a reality greater than itself. So, when speaking or thinking about God, this word is most inclusive. After all, it encompasses the following: omnipresent; everywhere; ever present; worldwide; Catholic or universal; in all places; all over; far and wide; right and left; throughout the length and breadth of the land; here, there, and everywhere; cosmic; even galactic!

What, therefore, does the word *ubiquitous* say about God? It proclaims that God is never limited by any spatial boundaries. Far from being a frightening concept, the notion of a transcendent deity is truly good news for each of us. This means that there is no place where the love, grace, and justice of God do not extend. The writers of the sacred scriptures attempt to help us understand this fact: "The Most High does not dwell in houses made with human hands" (Acts 7:48 NRSV). In other words, God does not reside merely within the sanctity of the stained-glass windows of the church (not even the great cathedrals). God is present and active among Christians, Jews, Muslims, and even people of zero religious commitment. He is present and active in every tribe and nation of earth, with all races, all economic and social classes, and all cultures. Perhaps the ancient poet says it best:

> Whither shall I go from thy Spirit?
> Or whither shall I flee from thy presence?
> If I ascend to heaven, thou art there!

If I make my bed in Sheol, thou
art there! (Psalm 139:7–8 NRSV)

It becomes clear that the individual who believes in the *ubiquitous God of Abraham, Moses, and Jesus* is positioned to affirm the efficacy of global prayer. In this sense, the family of God—all of us human beings— is liberated to talk with our heavenly Father simultaneously. Further, the diverse petitions of the Father's diverse children claim the divine attention of the Father, and they are attentively received, evaluated, and answered. All of this is real because God the Father Almighty is *ubiquitous.*

Selah!

# VIRGIN BIRTH

The words *virgin birth* constitute the ultimate test of orthodoxy for many evangelical Christians. In contemporary language, this is the declaration that it was the Holy Spirit and not Joseph who got Mary pregnant. While I am not prepared to reject as false this cherished faith component, neither am I prepared to insist that the advent of Jesus had to have been by way of a virgin birth. Certainly, it is biblically accurate to observe that our salvation is actualized by the events at the end of Jesus's life rather than the event at the beginning.

It remains quite interesting that the writer of our earliest gospel makes no reference to the virgin birth. The great apostle Paul, likewise, never mentions the virgin birth in his many writings. It is inconceivable to think that if such an unprecedented event had occurred, mention of it would have been ignored by the likes of Mark, John, Paul, Peter, James, and the writer of Hebrews. On one occasion, Paul did observe that "God was in Christ reconciling the world unto himself" (2 Corinthians 5:19 NRSV). If we are able to accept as gospel the notion that God was in Christ, does it really make any difference how he got there?

In a word, it is not inherent in biblical theology to affirm a given doctrine merely for the sake of the doctrine itself. Rather it is essential to strive to comprehend the person, purpose, and meaning of Jesus. Therefore, the birth narratives of Matthew and Luke provide us with the incalculably valuable insight that in Jesus we have "God with us" (Matthew 1:23 NRSV). In other words, the advent is infinitely more than some abstract theological concept. Indeed, it is an event that happened! And that makes of it the concrete and validated stuff of history.

Let us attempt an additional observation about the virgin birth. The person, teachings, mission, and ministry of Jesus remain unique in the unfolding saga of the human story. If, indeed, he is to be viewed as unique, we may conclude that genetics, heredity, and environment played no role in his life and contribution. It seems that his ideas and actions were free from the restraint of flawed human influence. The sacred scriptures meticulously instruct us regarding the evolutionary nature of sin and evil. In contrast, Jesus is righteous holiness that happens! It seems to me that we cannot rule out the possibility of the virgin birth.

# WORSHIP

The word *worship* has to do with a subject with which we *all* are familiar. Further, we all know exactly what *worship* is. Right? After all, we *all* worship in the same manner on the same day and use the same images, music, and liturgy. And we *all* endure the same age-old practice of sitting still while somebody attempts to instill (otherwise known as *preaching*). Such is hardly the case! There is quite a contrast between the dynamic Pentecostal congregation and the staid and stilted procedures of the mainstream formal creedal church. Yet both religious expressions are termed *worship* by the respective participants.

Let us consider the matter from another perspective. Is the word *worship* to be understood as a verb or a noun? Is it intended to describe an action or an event? Or both? In other words, is *worship* something we do or something we attend? Well, perhaps we will profit by looking at each in turn.

Let us think of worship as a religious lifestyle. I suppose that this involves a certain functional attitude. There are some persons who are convinced that they engage in authentic worship when they care for the widows and orphans in their affliction, visit those who are in prison or the hospital, and give a financial donation to the Salvation Army every Christmas. That must be what James had in mind when he suggested that *faith without works is dead.* So, our *busy work* exists as a tangible evidence of our faith. And why not? When reflecting in this manner, it may be said that *worship is what we do for God.*

What about worship as an event? We all know about such events. We assemble for the scheduled worship service. Much effort is given these days to be certain that we are inclusive of all opinions. So, we advertise our *traditional worship,* and we advertise our *contemporary worship.* The respective techniques may vary broadly, but the essential components are consistent: songs, scriptures, prayers, affirmations of one sort or another, and some kind of homily, sermon, or discussion. Why the differences? It may well be that *worship as an event is what we do for ourselves.* And since we all are different, we choose to worship differently. What is wrong with that?

Any way you look at it, the word *worship* has to do with the meaningful communication between a human being and the Almighty. Sometimes it is achieved through worshipful actions of service to others. Sometimes it is achieved through established formal and/or informal expressions of praise, adoration, and sermon. Frankly, I doubt that God is keeping score on which way dominates our lives. Surely, he is pleased that his children worship him, in whatever way.

# ZION

The congregation stands to sing the hymn of praise during the Sunday morning worship service. The song remains one of the favorites of many Christians. It is entitled "O Zion, Haste." The lyrics and hymn tune blend perfectly for enthusiastic participation. Recall the words of that stirring song:

> O Zion, haste, thy mission high fulfilling,
> to tell to all the world that God is light,
> that he who made all nations is not willing
> one soul should perish, lost in shades of night.
> Publish glad tidings, tidings of peace;
> tidings of Jesus, redemption and release.

Good song! But what is meant by the word *Zion?* In the evolving saga of the salvation history as presented in the Bible, Zion may be understood as both a place and a symbol. Located between the Kidron and Tyropoean valleys, there is a triangular plateau that emerges above the surrounding plains. It is a natural fortress enhanced by abundant natural water supply from the Gihon Spring on its eastern border. Located near the center of this plateau was a fortress named Ophel. It is likely that this is what was identified as the *Stronghold of Zion:*

> Then Solomon assembled the elders of Israel and all the heads of the tribes, the leaders of the fathers' houses of the people of Israel, before King Solomon in Jerusalem, to bring up the ark of the covenant of the Lord out of the city of David, which is Zion. (1 Kings 8:1 NRSV)

> And David and all Israel went to Jerusalem, that is Jebus, where the Jebusites were. the inhabitants of the land. The inhabitants of Jebus said to David, "You will not come in

here." Nevertheless David took the stronghold of Zion, that is, the city of David. (1 Chronicles 11:4–5 NRSV)

So it is clear that Zion is to be perceived as geographical. But it is far more. The word *Zion* embodies the very spirit of the people of God. Frequently characterized as a woman, Zion might writhe as a mother, suffer the crime of rape, or emerge as a feminist protestor (Micah 4:8–13). The book of Lamentations presents her as a gentle mourner. In the Jewish apocalyptic chronicles, Zion is identified as the mother who welcomes her suffering children into a transcendent world. We are familiar with that messianic image in which Zion is symbolic of the kingdom of God on earth in which all peoples "shall beat their swords into plowshares, and their spears into pruning hooks; nation shall not lift up sword against nation, neither shall they learn war any more" (Micah 4; Isaiah 2).

The Christian Church has carried forward the eschatological notions born in the Hebrew mentality. Indeed, the church is viewed as the new Zion on earth, for the kingdom of God is present (Mark 1:15; Matthew 12:28, etc.). Accordingly, Christians look for the consummation of this kingdom in a heavenly Zion, which is perceived as being imminent (Revelation 14).

# PART 4

## Epilogue:

# AN APOLOGIA OF THE EVOLUTION OF A BELIEVER'S PILGRIMAGE

# EPILOGUE

A rather strange phenomenon has evolved in my life. I have grown into old age chronologically, and into young ideas and dreams at the same time. Actually, it is quite interesting to realize that the inevitable accumulating of the years does not equate with the burgeoning concepts and stratagems that flood the mind. Specifically, I have become captive to the notion that the exercise of reverent faith and intellectual curiosity opens the channels of the mind and spirit for an ever-enlarging awareness of the universal verities that we are born to experience. Of course, I realize that we are born infants, and we grow through the experiences of living and learning into progressive maturity. Just as the firm foundation of the house is of comparable importance to the rafters, beams, and roof, so our initial steps toward authentic religious conviction are of similar significance to those later steps of philosophical and theological discoveries.

I am grateful to God for the priceless gift of memory. Actually, the privilege of remembering is one of the primary rewards of old age. I find myself relishing the memory of the home and family into which I was born. I grew up in the home with my mother, grandfather, grandmother, and aunt. Due to factors that I shall not discuss here, it became necessary for my mother to divorce my father when I was about two years of age. Frankly, I do not know very much about those mitigating circumstances. They were never discussed in my presence. But I thrived in the loving and supportive environs of life with my mother (Elizabeth Nolen Holland), grandfather (Furman Jutson Nolen), grandmother (Hannah Williams Nolen), and aunt (Gladys). It was a simple, humble, Christian home. The "Jesus Book" was read to me frequently. We were always in attendance in the Baptist church where my family were members. I cannot remember when I did not believe in Jesus Christ as my Savior. I made a public profession of faith in Jesus Christ as my personal Savior, joined the church, and was baptized when I was eleven years of age.

There is no way to measure the profound contribution to my faith in God, which was provided to me by my mother and grandparents. They were simple folk who possessed a noncritical and somewhat simplistic faith in God, the Bible and, the church. Devoted to a very conservative interpretation of the Bible and to a provincial style of living, my family provided me a morally, socially, and religiously circumscribed environment in which to develop. As an only child in a family of adults, I often had many hours to devise activities to my own liking. Very early in life, I discovered the compelling attraction of books. With scarcely enough money to make ends meet, as they say, my mother always found ways to provide me with the many books I loved to read. Literature became my great escape. Through reading, I traveled to distant lands in long-ago times and sat at the Round Table with the knights of King Arthur. Later, the epic stories of Greek mythology captured my attention. In it all, my very favorite writer was Alfred Lord Tennyson. However, I must not ignore the countless stories of the Old West, with its fascinating legends of cowboys, Indians, and the romantic stories of the US Cavalry, which claimed many of my boyhood summer days. Indeed, the lifelong love affair with books that has enriched my life was begun in that simpler time and place made possible for me by a mother and grandparents who surrounded me with unconditional love.

Then a strange thing happened to me on the way to manhood. I met a girl! Jeanette Crowder was that girl! It is difficult now for me to recall a time when I did not know Jeanette. We grew up in the same community, attended the same church, and graduated from the same high school. She must have been about twelve years old the first time I ever really noticed her. It was an Easter Sunday morning, and I was standing in a Sunday school classroom, looking out the window. Her family car was driven into the parking lot of the church, and a little girl dressed in a beautiful white dress stepped out of the car. It struck me that day that she was the prettiest girl I had ever seen. (Incidentally, she still is the prettiest girl I have ever seen.)

Although I have never forgotten that seminal moment of long ago, it was several years before I succeeded in securing more than a casual relationship with Jeanette. In the interim, I proceeded into the teen years with the usual attractions and distractions of the average high school boy. There were those hesitant, and sometimes not so hesitant, efforts of flirtation with that bewildering species of the opposite sex. Jeanette is three years younger than I, so our paths did not cross often during the high school years. Fortunately for me, there never was another girl with whom I established any kind of lasting interest. Of course, there were fun times and interesting experiences along the way, but I am convinced that God was guiding me through the sometimes confusing web of adolescent pressures and circumstances to the one person with whom he had destined me to spend my life.

In the providence of God, Jim Crowder, Jeanette's brother, and I became very close friends. We took several classes together in school, were in the same Sunday school class, and were usually found together on those weekend activities. We graduated high school, took different jobs, and still we remained very close friends. At the time, I was employed by the Atlanta Gas and Light Company. Jim worked with his father in their grocery store. One day, Jim asked me if I would help them in the store on Saturdays. So, I took that job. Jim and I enjoyed working together each Saturday. We took several vacations together, once to Gatlinburg and, another time, to Florida. Then something happened that interrupted our constant companionship.

About the time Jeanette was fifteen years old, I saw her again! This time, I really saw her! That pretty little girl in the white dress had grown into the loveliest girl in the community. Of course, I was determined to do her a great favor and allow her to give me a date. I thought she would jump at that idea! For some strange reason, she was somewhat cool to the thought. To this day, I have difficulty understanding her hesitancy in realizing what a great opportunity she was missing. But time passed, and my obsession with her intensified. Ultimately, when she became sixteen years old (about the time I became nineteen), as a result of my persistence and gentle persuasion, she finally surrendered to my implorations. We started dating then, and we have been dating ever since.

Although neither of us was aware of the other's spiritual struggles during those days, God was working in each of our lives. To be very candid about the matter, God was preparing us to enter the ministry. The very thought was disconcerting to us respectively, and, yet, we did not quickly share with each other what we were experiencing. After a period of time, the opportunity presented itself for us to discuss our future together. Gradually, we came to realize that God was calling us into special Christian service. On June 7, 1953, Jeanette and I were married. Through the succeeding years, we attended college together and on through graduate school as well. I will summarize this development with as strong affirmation as I am capable: the primary influence in my life in the preparation for and exercise of the Christian ministry has been the bride of my youth, my Jeanette.

Now that the subject of the ministry has emerged, this is a good point to state with emphasis that I am convinced that the Christian ministry is the ultimately important calling that can come to any person. It is never an easy occupation. It is not a profession that assures great financial benefits. It is a service that is sometimes respected, often ignored or tolerated in certain social circles, and, sadly, frequently subjected to painful rejection and suffering. Nevertheless, it is for me the grandest privilege in the world, because to be God's prophet is to be God's means of communicating his love and salvation to all people. After sixty years of trying to be a faithful preacher of the Word, I think that if God had not called me to preach the gospel, I would apply for the job!

St. Thomas Aquinas points out that before we can seek the means of satisfying God's expectations of us, we must be convinced of what he expects of us. Following our mutual surrendering to the call of God in our lives, Jeanette and I became convinced that God expected us to make adequate and proper educational preparation for the task to which he had called us. We knew that if such preparation were made, our goal of satisfying God's expectation would be enhanced greatly. This thought introduces the role of theological education in the development of any effective and relevant minister.

The university experience was, for me, a life-changing process. Upon entering Mercer University, I arrived with the biblical orientation that had been provided in Sunday school classes throughout my childhood and adolescent years. I came with an audacious confidence in the literal accuracy of every word, event, and concept recorded in the scriptures. The notion of any form of critical analysis was foreign to my provincial mentality. Jeanette shares the same recollection of her own introduction into the expanding world of academia. It was there, in Mercer University, that the miracle of intellectual rebirth took place. I received the Bachelor of Arts degree (BA) from Mercer University. It pleases me that Jeanette is also an alumnus of Mercer. Therefore, we share beautiful memories together of those days when we really were roommates in college!

The dominant influence in my years in university study was Dr. G. McCloud Bryan, professor of philosophy. It was during his provocative lectures that the shell of limited sectarian bias was cracked. It was there that I was introduced to those giants of reflective reason and logic. Aristotle and Plato became lights in the darkness of limited and circumscribed intellectual rigidity. I was privileged to walk with the likes of Augustine, Socrates, Kant, Spinoza, Descartes, James, and Hume. It was there that the spirit was liberated from the narrow prison of prejudice, tradition, and social and political indifference. To express the experience in evangelical terms, it was at Mercer University that I was born again into a world where essential truth transcends all traditions, dogmas, and assumed religious and intellectual limitations. There, the words of Jesus blossomed with relevance: "You will know the truth, and the truth will make you free" (John 8:32 NRSV).

It was, however, during the years of graduate study in seminary that I discovered the passion of my life: biblical theology. I owe a debt of gratitude to some of the great teachers of the faculty of the Southern Baptist Theological Seminary. I recall, in particular, Dr. Eric Rust, professor of philosophy of religion, and Dr. Dale Moody, professor of theology. With their soaring intellects, they revealed the remarkable relationship of philosophy and theology. This emphasis remained a primary focus of my interest, research, and preaching throughout my ministry. I received the bachelor of divinity (BD) degree from Southern Seminary. Dr. Rust became a friend with whom I retained communication through the years.

In retrospect, the greatest contribution to the evolving process of theological education for me was the Columbia Theological Seminary of

Decatur, Georgia. This splendid Presbyterian institution came to be the spiritual and academic foundation of my life. It was in Columbia that I came under the influence of such towering Christian gentlemen and scholars as Dr. Samuel A. Cartledge, Dr. Ludwig DeWitz, Dr. Manford George Gutzke, Dr. William Childs Robinson, Dr. J. McDowell Richards, Dr. Felix Gear, Dr. Shirley Guthrie, and Dr. Charles Cousar. Dr. DeWitz would chair the faculty committee that guided my studies for the master of theology degree (ThM). Dr. Cartledge was my mentor for the doctor of theology degree (ThD).

Dr. DeWitz was a remarkably gifted scholar who was fluent in five languages. As a young Jewish student, he came to accept Jesus as Messiah, and became one of the premier scholars in America in the area of Hebrew and Arabic languages. It was from him that I gained an awareness and appreciation for the study of salvation history as it evolved in the continuing saga of Israel. My thesis emphasis under Dr. DeWitz gives evidence of his influence. It is entitled *The Theological Significance of the Images of God in the Old Testament*. It was during the time spent in this effort that my awareness of the progressive evolution of the self-revelation of God in the Old Testament began to take shape. My personal perception of the Almighty grew and matured in the process, just as the perception of the prophets and poets of ancient Israel grew with the passing of the years. The imagery of the narratives, prophetic oracles, and poetry of the Hebrew sensibility has continued to enrich and inspire my own spiritual formulations. Needless to say, through the many years of sermon preparation and presentation, I constantly have returned again and again to the mine of Hebrew gold found in the mountains of truth within the Old Testament.

There does not exist sufficient time and space in which to relate the extent of influence Dr. Samuel A. Cartledge had on my life. He was the professor of Literature, Language, and Exegesis of the New Testament, and he was dean of the graduate school. He was widely recognized as one of the leading scholars in the discipline of the Greek New Testament. Under his direction, I was led to exegete from the Greek New Testament the entire books of the Gospel of John, James, Philippians, and the Revelation. As we worked through the texts, the commentary of Dr. Cartledge opened the fountains of redemptive truth that became virtual streams of hermeneutical insight for me.

During the days of my ThD efforts, he made it possible for me to collate portions of the Gospel of Mark from copies of the Dead Sea Scrolls (truly a stimulating moment in my studies).

As profoundly significant in my academic life as was Dr. Cartledge, his personal friendship through the succeeding years remained one of the most important relationships of my entire life. His personal interest in me, and his love for my wife and children, enriched our lives in countless ways. For years, I invited him to come as guest lecturer in the churches where I served as pastor. During those times, he shared with us as a member of our family. So it is that Samuel A. Cartledge, brilliant scholar and a true Presbyterian gentleman, lives in my memory as one of the premier Christian influences in my life. His insistence on thorough research, study, and the pursuit of excellence in the proclamation of the truth remains the essential objective of my ministry.

The perimeters of this effort do not favor a lengthy recitation of all of the remarkable personalities who have invaded my experience with their invaluable insights, encouragement, counsel, and examples. Yet, they pass through the corridors of my memory on a regular basis. That roll call of significant influences must include such persons as Mrs. Polly Evans (my high school literature teacher), Dr. James P. Wesberry, and Dr. Louie D. Newton.

From time to time over the years, I have had the opportunity to serve as adjunct professor in several seminaries. Always, this proved to be an altogether rewarding experience for me. There were two occasions when I was approached about a teaching position in the seminary. In the first instance, I had just accepted the call of a large church to become their pastor, and ethical and pecuniary considerations influenced my declining the offer. In the second instance, certain members among the trustees of that institution raised the question of my theological views, actually suggesting that I was far too liberal to teach on that faculty. Of course, there have been times when I have reflected on what might have been. I think that I would have enjoyed a life of cloistered study, writing, and teaching. However, at this point, my Presbyterian tendency emerges. I truly believe that "all things work together for good for those who love God, who are called according to his purpose" (Romans 8:28 NRSV). I suppose that I am stating that I was *predestined* to be a preacher of the gospel to the people of God in congregations of God's choosing.

The moment has arrived when I must speak of some of those splendid pastors in my life whose love and assistance paved the way to a long and meaningful pastoral ministry. There were two men who served as pastor in churches where I attended with my family who contributed much to my life. Rev. W.S. Pruitt, a good and godly shepherd of the flock, expressed a great interest in me when I was but a boy. It was under his kind and patient guidance that I made public my faith in Jesus Christ, joined the North Side Park Baptist Church, and was baptized. An unlettered, but wise and competent preacher, Rev. Pruitt set the example of the truly devoted pastor. As I entered into the teenage years, my family moved into the Center Hill community, and we joined the Center Hill Baptist Church. Shortly thereafter, Rev. Joseph W. Head arrived as the pastor. As Jeanette and I reached the point of surrendering to the call of God to the ministry, Rev. Head was of significant encouragement and help, driving us to Mercer University himself and introducing us to Dr. Spright Dowell, the president. Of course, I shall always remember with fondness that Rev. Head officiated at our wedding ceremony.

It would be possible to write an entire book on the many contributions that the churches I have served have made to our lives. I recall with great gratitude and love those first small rural churches that opened their homes and hearts to us. Throughout our college and seminary years, we had the privilege of serving some of the finest congregations in the country. We began this pilgrimage in the churches when Jeanette was nineteen years old and I was twenty-two. As burgeoning neophytes in the awesome arena of "doing church," we coupled the rigors of academia and pastoral responsibility with enthusiastic alacrity and a positive attitude. Untrained, academically unprepared, and profoundly inexperienced, we joyfully entered the ministry with a certain confidence that we were obeying the call of God in our lives. Thank God for the love and support of Union Hill and Bethany Baptist churches, where we began our pastoral odyssey. In spite of our impetuous energy, constant experiment with new and radical ideas, and an occasional lapse of judgment, those dear members embraced our youth and inexperience with patience, love, and unfailing support. Down the corridor of memory there march the inspiring images of men, women, and youth who shared in the making of a minister.

There have been others—many others! For example, the wonderful Lewisport Baptist Church in Lewisport, Kentucky, comes to mind. We journeyed there with a seven-month- old baby, our little Denise, for the purpose of entering the Southern Baptist Theological Seminary. Once again, we found ourselves surrounded by a cordial congregation of encouraging, affirming, and loving members. They seemed to take great pleasure in helping us raise the little one. The faces of Emerson and Rachael Young come to mind when we think of Lewisport, for they received us into their home and family, and they continued to maintain that strong bond of love through the years to come. It was while in Lewisport that our second little angel, Alicia Doreen, was born. Our members rejoiced in the fact that one of our children forever would remain a native-born Kentuckian. We too are proud of that fact.

Our first church after seminary days was the First Baptist Church of Austell, Georgia. Again, we found ourselves encompassed by a cloud of younger, ambitious, upwardly mobile people who enjoyed life and enjoyed their church experience as well. Austell was a suburban community on the outskirts of Atlanta, so we enjoyed the delightful opportunities available in the big city while we shared in the close community sensibility prevalent in our church area. There were many splendid lessons taught to me regarding the pastoral and administrative responsibilities essential in the local church setting, lessons that only experience can provide. Once again, dedicated laymen were supportive and generous with their time and talents. Indeed, those three years were exciting times of evangelistic outreach, congregational building, and personal maturation. It was while serving the First Baptist Church of Austell that our third daughter, Beth, was born. She was then, and continues to be, a delight to our family.

It would be a personally satisfying experience if I were to take the time and space to chronicle the highlights in each of the churches where we have served. I suppose that our years with Capitol View Baptist Church in Atlanta, Georgia, were some of the very best. At any rate, that is the church our daughters remember with warmest feeling.

I am pleased that their formative years were spent in such a dynamic spiritual environment. It was the Capitol View congregation that made possible my continuing study. By unanimous vote of the deacons, I was urged to return to seminary and earn the coveted doctor's degree. Thus, for five years, Capitol View supported my academic efforts with prayer and financial provision. Indeed, they made it possible for me to earn both the ThM and ThD degrees from the beloved Columbia Theological Seminary. Think of it! A Baptist church sponsoring their pastor to advanced degrees in a Presbyterian seminary! Thus, I became heir to an ecumenical sensibility that has enriched my life and ministry. Frankly, this diverse educational orientation did not retain a universal approval among all of my Baptist constituents, and often it contributed to my being theologically suspect to many.

Through the years, I have had the opportunity to serve some wonderful congregations in small, medium, and large churches. Our ministry has taken us to Georgia, Tennessee, Kentucky, Washington DC, North Carolina, and Texas. There were times when the experience was altogether exciting and fulfilling. There were times when the situations were disappointing and even failures. In retrospect, I can detect the presence and guidance of God throughout the process.

The Southern Baptist Convention was the denomination in which and to which we had given our lives in love and service. In 1979, a shift in philosophical and theological perspective began to unfold in the Convention. A highly organized strategy to purge the Convention of all elements of "liberal persuasion" became actualized. It began to spread across the denomination like some great ideological tidal wave. It seemed to me at the time that every semblance of scholarly and intellectual enquiry was sacrificed on the altar of rigid theological conformity. Such a non-thinking mentality was repulsive to my ecumenical orientation. Neither I nor my wife felt at peace in the environs of our religious home. Nevertheless, for several years, I continued to serve as pastor. However, the tensions and unrest were mounting for both myself and the congregation as well. Increasingly, my views and positions became matters of debate and subsequent confusion. I am certain, as I evaluate my participation in the process, that I failed to adjust my response to the challenges of the time with maturity and dignity. In retrospect, I could have done better than I did!

172

The time came when I could no longer sustain the tenuous balance between personal philosophical and theological conviction and established congregational expectation. Thus, in January 1990, I resigned from the pastorate. What could I do now? For thirty-eight years, I had been a Baptist pastor. What does a Baptist pastor do when he no longer is a Baptist pastor? Consequently, I found myself drifting for several months, trying to find myself and become oriented to a new order of things in my life. For a period of time, I tried my hand with a church stewardship organization, guiding congregations in their fundraising efforts. This proved to be for me a "striving after the wind" endeavor: busy and yet meaningless. How long could I maintain this charade?

Then a phone call came from my long-time friend, Mickey Wesmoreland of Atlanta, Georgia. This outstanding business leader had a proposal for me. He wanted to establish an organization for the purpose of preparing Christian literature appropriate for all denominations. Further, he wanted me to lead the new organization. Thus, the Biblical Studies Association was born. The administrative office was in Atlanta, and the ministry office was in Fort Worth. Mr. Wesmoreland was president of the enterprise, and I was designated vice president and executive director. My task was to prepare and publish the desired literature, and engage in raising the needed funds for meeting operating expenses. This endeavor made possible for Jeanette and me the experience of an enlarged fellowship of Christians. Accordingly, we traveled through much of the eastern area of the country, focusing particularly on the Theological Consortium of New England. This enabled us to visit such institutions as Andover-Newton Theological School, Harvard Divinity School, and Boston College. As a result of this effort, I was able to publish the book *Christianity for Tomorrow,* including the work of some of New England's finest scholars in the process, along with my own contribution.

Then another phone call came—a call that was destined to change my life dramatically. Bishop William R. Canon of the United Methodist Church called. Initially, we began discussing the possibility of his contributing another essay to a book I was planning. Suddenly, he said to me a very surprising statement, "Charles, I believe you should return to the pulpit. Your voice and message are greatly needed at this time."

Somewhat stunned by the directness of his proposition, I replied, "Bishop Canon, I cannot buy a pulpit in the Southern Baptist Convention today."

Then, Bishop Canon said, "I know that, son. But I was not thinking of the Southern Baptist Convention. I was speaking of the United Methodist Church." He continued, "Charles, if the door were to open for you to enter the Methodist Church, would you walk through it?"

I replied, "No, Bishop Canon, I would not walk through it. I would run through it." Two days later, I was appearing before the Board of Ordained Ministry of the South Georgia Conference of the United Methodist Church. The very next day, I was appointed as an associate pastor on the staff of the First United Methodist Church of Bainbridge, Georgia.

Then, for ten years, I had the privilege of serving as pastor of some very fine churches. First to the Avalon United Methodist Church of Albany, Georgia, and then, in order, I served the Benbrook United Methodist Church and Polytechnic United Methodist Church of Fort Worth, Texas. These churches were wonderful opportunities, and we enjoyed our time with them very much. The ministry in the Polytechnic congregation took on a special opportunity. I was asked by Bishop Joe Wilson to guide the church into merging into the Texas Wesleyan University. I prepared a Paradigm for Merger, and after three years, the church became an intrinsic entity with the university.

In 2002, Jeanette and I retired from our respective assignments. Jeanette completed about thirty years as a teacher in public schools, and I completed fifty years as a pastor. The intervening time has proven to be a process of learning to adjust to life off center stage. Yet, these have been years of significant contribution on our part as well. For a number of years, Jeanette has responded to the call by various schools to provide special instruction for elementary and middle school students in the area of language arts. This has been a personally fulfilling and satisfying experience for her.

During this ten-year period, I have had opportunity to serve a number of churches in an intentional interim pastor role. These appointments have included the Runaway Bay Community Church in Bridgeport, Texas, and congregations in Lufkin, San Saba, and Crawford, Texas. It should be noted here that Jeanette and I had the opportunity to organize and constitute a new church in San Saba (The Church of the Open Door). On one occasion, I served a three-month interim for the Eastern Hills Baptist Church of Fort Worth. Significantly, I enjoyed a three-year ministry as the stated pastor of the Wesley United Methodist Church of Fort Worth. More recently, I served a seven-month interim pastorate in the First United Methodist Church of Coleman, Texas. As such opportunities open for me, I continue to make every effort to engage each respective situation with as diligent study preparation and pulpit presentation as I offered through the many years of pastoral ministry. Remaining theologically oriented and intellectually relevant to the present social, political, and moral issues facing this generation remains the priority objective of my continuing ministry.

At the time of this writing, I am completing twenty years as an elder in the United Methodist Church. At various times, I have been asked to describe the differences I have encountered in the Methodist Church when contrasted to the years in the Baptist ministry. To be honest with you, the contrast is not so prominent as the similarities. I have discovered that people are essentially the same, no matter their respective religious structures. To paraphrase Sir Winston Churchill, people forever strive to structure their institutions, and forever, thereafter, their institutions structure them. So it is in the world of organized (and sometimes quite disorganized) religion. In significant measure, we become captive to some system, and through the processes of a sanctified form of deductive reasoning, we buttress the perimeters of our own personal and collective security and power base. So it is that in all ecclesiastical groupings of which I have knowledge, the ministry of administration is often sought by many of us in preference to the actual ministry of the cross and the towel. I am prepared to hear the voices of protestation regarding this notion. I too am schooled in the academy of P.R.A.—that is Planning, Research, and Action. And after all, someone must administer the planning and research if the action is to have any success. Right?

Such thinking as this tends to leave one pondering the future of established religious institutions at every level. I once heard someone observe that the primary malaise of the church is the paralysis of analysis. If this analysis has any merit, perhaps we should be aware of a plethora of emerging issues:

1. Is the established church, with its prevailing systems mentality, retaining any significant relevance?

2. To what extent is the church losing its unique identity as the authentic embodiment of the divine Presence in the world?

3. Is it reasonable to ask the question, "Does the church have a future?"

4. Is the current trend of designing the liturgy and worship formations of the church into a contemporary presentation really a drastic method of creating a religion in our own image rather than in the image of the sovereign and transcendent Holy Other? If such is the case to any measurable extent, is this not merely the process of self-adoration and worship? I wonder!

5. Do we have the courage to engage in the critical theological investigation of what the church, as perceived from its origin, essentially and authentically is?

At first glance, these observations may appear to emerge from the convoluted sensibility of a convinced pessimist. However, these are merely cautionary comments from the existential concerns of an authentic religious optimist. I remain persuaded of the ultimate victory of the church in its perennial conflict with the daunting forces of secularism, materialism, and social and political power. Indeed, I am captive to the rapture of the forward look regarding the church, and this optimistic pronouncement is based on the powerful words of our Lord: "I will build *my* Church, and the powers of death shall not prevail against it" (Matthew16:18 NRSV).

Our confidence in the future of the church is based on the fact that it is Christ's church. The future of the church is not dependent on the Baptist, Methodist, Presbyterian, Episcopalian, Catholic, or any other sectarian grouping. Indeed, since it is Christ's church, it will remain relevant, right, and redemptive in any and all evolving circumstances of the human saga if the gospel of Jesus Christ remains the essential criterion of the church's life. It remains difficult to perpetually recall that the church, as intended by Jesus Christ, is to be perceived not as an organization, but as an organism. I still recall William Childs Robinson, professor of historical theology in Columbia Theological Seminary, making the following observation: "The historical development of the Church has been a movement from vital groups to more organized and less vital organizations."

I grieve the present state of organized religion amid the political, economic, social, and international challenges of our time. Still, I do not ascribe to the notion that we are witness to the certain demise of the church as the redemptive leaven in the loaf of human complexity. In time, I believe that we shall see the growth of a pattern of "doing church" more akin to the experience of the New Testament believers. By this, I mean that we shall observe the essential components of first-century Christianity becoming the integrating center of our corporate Christian experience rather than the structured systems and organizational paradigm common among most denominations today. It seems to me that those revived and emerging essential components are composed of the following:

1. **Witness:** The primary mission of the church is *witness*. It was the reality and power of the witness of the first Christians that gave and sustained the life of the believers in the first century. It was the witness of Peter on the Day of Pentecost that ignited the flame that continues to glow even to this very day.

2. **Service:** Born in the teaching and example of Jesus and affirmed in the strong emphasis of Paul, the primacy of service dominates the life of first-century Christianity. When the church truly is vital and relevant, service to God and others is the central focus.

3. **Fellowship:** Following the event of Pentecost, fellowship existed as the singular unifying factor in the life of the church. Nowhere is the importance of fellowship better explained than in 1 John 1:3–4 (NRSV):

177

That which we have seen and heard
we are proclaiming to you,
in order that you may have fellowship with us;
and our fellowship is with the Father
and with his son Jesus Christ;
and these things we are writing to you
in order that your joy may be complete.

In summary, I remain convinced that the future for the church, the gospel, and the redemptive ministries of authentic Christianity are as bright as the promises of God. Absolutely, I place my faith in Jesus, who made a promise to the witnessing, serving, and loving church: "I am with you always, to the close of the age" (Matthew 28:20 NRSV). Speaking of the closing of the age, I conclude these remarks with that sublime affirmation of St. Augustine:

Suffice it to say that the seventh (age) shall be our Sabbath, which shall be brought to a close, not by an evening, but by the Lord's day, as an eighth and eternal day, consecrated by the resurrection of Christ and prefiguring the eternal repose not only of the spirit, but also of the body. There we shall rest and see, see and love, love and praise. This is what shall be in the end without end. For what other end do we propose to ourselves than to attain to the kingdom of which there is no end? (*City of God*, 20.30)

# ACKNOWLEDGMENTS

In the preparation and writing of this book, I have been encouraged by my daughters and their husbands: Denise and Michael Truncale, Alicia and Charles Daleo, and Beth and Andy Sims. Of course, the primary motivator in my every endeavor is my wife, Jeanette. Certainly such is the case in the production of this book.

I am most appreciative for the editing, typing, and often correcting of the manuscript, which Michael willingly contributed to the process. In addition, my grandson, Jonathan, and my granddaughter, Heather, have been of great value in the final editing process, and I am most grateful for their assistance. Of course, I would be remiss if I were to fail to thank the several congregations and classes where I have fieldtested parts 2 and 3 of the book. It was in those instances and settings that I came to realize that the material included did indeed serve as instructive and dialogical incentive. Again, the feedback from the participants in those experiences has underscored the relevance of the effort.

In the issuance of this second edition of LOOKING AHEAD, I have received significant encouragement, counsel, and advise from Felicity Anderson. Her patience with my lengthy and often confusing deliberations has been tested. I am grateful to her for her willingness to persevere.

Lightning Source UK Ltd.
Milton Keynes UK
UKHW011127291119
354427UK00003BA/110/P